March Forward with the Word!

The Life of Conrad Grebel

March Forward with the Word!

The Life of Conrad Grebel

Andrew V. Ste. Marie
Mike Atnip

SERMON ON THE MOUNT
PUBLISHING
Manchester, MI

ISBN 978-1-68001-006-0
Library of Congress Control Number: 2016911606

For additional titles and other material by the same authors, contact:

Sermon on the Mount Publishing
P.O. Box 246
Manchester, MI 48158
(734) 428-0488
the-witness@sbcglobal.net
www.kingdomreading.com

Our Mission
To obey the commands of Christ and to teach men to do so.

About the Cover
The front cover is a representation of the very first Anabaptist baptism, in the home of Felix Manz's mother, January 21, 1525. Conrad Grebel is shown standing, baptizing Georg Blaurock, while Felix Manz looks on. On the back cover, Wilhelm Reublin and Felix's mother are praying while the baptism is performed.
Scene conceived by Andrew Ste. Marie; painted by Lisa Strubhar.

First Printing—August 2016—1045 copies
Second Printing—POD Edition
Third Printing—October 2018—1000 copies

Dedication

This series is dedicated to the Lord Jesus Christ,
the King of Saints.

This volume is also dedicated to Dale Heisey. It was his retelling of Anabaptist beginnings that sparked my interest in Anabaptist history. I was on the edge of my seat as he described Simon Stumpf's confrontation of Zwingli during the Second Zürich Disputation.
Thank you, my brother, for inspiring me!
~A.V.S.

Acknowledgements

The authors thank the many people who have contributed to this project in various ways. First, thanks and praise to the Lord Jesus Christ, King of Saints, inheritor of the Gentiles. May the entire earth bow before Him.

Vincent and Barbara Ste. Marie, Chester Weaver, and Dennis Lengacher read the manuscript and offered helpful suggestions. John D. Roth, C. Arnold Snyder, and the Christian Light Publications staff gave helpful suggestions and comments; Leon Yoder was particularly helpful. Lisa Strubhar did an excellent job painting the illustration for the front cover. Peter Balholm gave invaluable help in the process of doing the historical research for the painting. Rod & Staff Publishers allowed us the use of the illustration of Andreas Castelberger. MennoMedia and the Mennonite Historical Society granted permission to use the many quotations from their translations of primary sources. Jennifer Burdge copyedited the manuscript. Thank you all for making this book possible. An additional thanks to all those who gave an encouraging word as we worked through this project. May the Lord Jesus be glorified.

Cross Bearers

Series

The **Cross Bearers Series** is presented to acquaint readers with men and women who followed in Jesus' steps. Today's reader is inundated with biographies of those who professed Christ, but who did not teach and practice what Jesus taught and practiced.

One of Jesus' plainest teachings is that "whosoever doth not bear his cross, and come after me, cannot be my disciple." (Luke 14:27) Yet how often we are told that Jesus died on the cross for us so that we do not need to die! Peter tells us in I Peter 2:21, "For even hereunto were ye called: because Christ also suffered for us, leaving us an example, that ye should follow his steps."

Our "heroes" help define who we are and who we intend to be. Today's youth are in desperate need of role models who go beyond saying, "Lord, Lord!" While Jesus is the Ultimate Example, we can also learn from those who strove to imitate Him. We can learn from their mistakes, as well as from their glorious victory over self, sin, Satan, and the world through the power of the Spirit that worked in them.

The stories presented in the *Cross Bearers Series* will be drawn from various ages and churches. While "historical fiction" may be easier to read, these biographies will present the stories using a minimum of author imagination. However, the stories will be salted and peppered with other content (artwork, photos, and text sidebars) to capture the context of the culture in which they walked.

The ultimate goal of the *Cross Bearers Series* is to provoke all of us to follow these men and women as they followed Christ.

Contents

Student and Sinner   1

Reformer's Aide   41

Disputation and Disillusionment   73

Development of a "Radical"   89

Missionary   123

Triumph Under Persecution   145

Bibliography   169

Illustration credits   171

1

Student and Sinner

He lived the life of many a little boy's dreams. His house was a castle, even if it was a smaller one. Swiss pikemen in funny, brightly-colored pants marched down the roads, armor glinting in the bright sun. Water as clear as glass lapped the shores of a lake just down the hill from his castle home. Green grasses waved their lanky heads in the soft breezes of June. Cattle lowed and kids—the goat kind—played their joyful antics among the rocks in the fields.

But not all was bright and fair. The rural cantons and the metropolitan cantons of the Swiss Confederacy were suspicious of each other and sometimes fought amongst themselves; all of them together feared and hated the Hapsburg (Holy Roman) Empire to the north. At any time, war could break out. Superstition abounded, with stories of dragons and haunted lakes that caused grievous hailstorms that beat the green grasses down. But beyond these fears was the stark reality of The Black Death. From seemingly nowhere, and at any time, the inhabitants of a town would begin to have strange swellings

Conrad's Zürich

The city that Conrad knew would hardly be called a city in today's terms—a mere 6000 people. The walled part of the city was only 94 acres, about the size of a nice Amish or Mennonite farm in the American Midwest.

The original settlers around Zürich were known as Helvetti, a Celtic people that were essentially one of the "wild" peoples who first wandered into Europe and eventually spread all the way from Ireland to Germany and south into France.

Zürich's recorded history began in Roman times, with a large structure being established on a little hill now called Lindenhof. Little islands built in the swampy areas at the end of the lake contained what was probably a temple. Oak logs were driven deep into the lakebed and a small structure built upon the logs. It is assumed that these structures were built above the lake level to deal with occasional flooding. With the lake on the south, the Limmat River on the east, and the Sihl River on the north and west, the Lindenhof had a natural defense system of swamps and rivers.

Zürich's spiritual history is dominated by the story of Felix and Regula. Felix and Regula were siblings, a part of the legendary Theban Legion. The story goes that the Roman Emperor Maximian sent his army to quell an uprising in what is now France, in 286 A.D. One of the legions was composed of Egyptian Christians, to the man. After the victory, the Emperor demanded that everyone should join in making sacrifices to the gods, as a celebration. The Theban Legion, although they had fought in the battle, refused the order, withdrawing from the celebrations.

Enraged, the Emperor demanded that the legion be decimated, meaning one of every ten soldiers be killed. If they refused to offer the sacrifices after that, they would be decimated again and again, until either they sacrificed, or none was left.

Zürich in Roman days

After the first decimation, the legion sent a letter to the Emperor explaining that they could not participate in idol worship. This so enraged the Emperor that he demanded the whole legion be killed immediately. However, some of the legion was scattered along the route to the battle site in various forts. Hearing of the killing, some of these individuals fled. Among those fleeing were Felix and Regula, with their servant, Exuperantius. Arriving at Zürich as refugees, they were caught, tried, and executed by decapitation. However, when their heads were chopped off, the three picked up their heads, walked 40 paces uphill, and prayed before finally dying.

The place where they died was the place the Grossmünster chapel would be built. Supposedly, the horse of the first Holy Roman Emperor, Charlemagne, fell to his knees over the graves of Felix and Regula.

How much of the above stories are true? No one really knows, since the stories were handed down verbally, or possibly contrived hundreds of years after the actual events. As followers of King Jesus, who has called us to beat our swords into plowshares, we do not get too excited about the story of Felix and Regula. What were they doing as soldiers in the first place? Should they not have refused military service, as lovers of peace, before even leaving Egypt?

Despite our misgivings of such stories, Conrad's Zürich would have held Felix, Regula, and Exuperantius up as saints to be emulated—and prayed to. The mass conversion of the local inhabitants in the days after the execution of the siblings and their servant has been attributed to their miraculous head carrying. Enthralled by the story, the local people by and large converted to Roman Catholicism. In Catholic, Coptic, and Orthodox churches, September 11 is still held as a feast day for the siblings.

ndenhof is on the right.

This heritage was part of what the early Anabaptists had to overcome in order to teach and live out the true gospel, which calls men and women out of military campaigns, and into a kingdom of peace, love, and joy. Some of the people who admired the story of Felix and Regula would be the very ones who would cut the heads off of the Anabaptists!

in their groins. The skin would turn black on parts of their bodies. Some would begin to cough up blood. Within days, most of them would die. Some small towns were literally depopulated by this unseen and unwelcome guest.

Young Conrad, born in Zurich, Switzerland, in about the year 1498, grew up in the midst of these contrasting medieval joys and sorrows. His parents, Jacob and Dorothea (Fries) Grebel, were part of the upper class in Zürich—one of the most powerful cantons in the Swiss Confederation. This son of the nobility was to change the course of history by renouncing his wealth and privilege to become an outcast. He would become one of the shakers and movers of a revival of authentic New Testament Christianity that spread across Europe like wildfire. The "Anabaptists," as they were derisively called by their enemies, went everywhere making disciples of the Lord Jesus. They would eventually gain strongholds in Switzerland, Germany, Holland, and Moravia. As the centuries rolled on, the movement would spread all around the globe, with tens of thousands of them in North America.

Conrad's Family

If a word is needed to describe the Grebel clan, that word is "prestige." The Grebel family was old stock, well-established in the canton of Zürich, one of the most powerful of all the cantons.[1] The family's residence in Zürich has been traced back to Lütold Grebel, who became a citizen of Zürich in 1386. From that day on, the Grebels were always a land-owning family and members of the patrician[2] guild in Zürich. From the time of Lütold's son Johannes, each generation of Grebels had one member as guildmaster. Simi-

---

1   The cantons were essentially city-states, but were all bound together in the Swiss Confederacy and participated in the Swiss Diet, which made non-binding decisions for the entire Confederacy.

2   Patricians were the upper-class citizens with the right to participate in politics.

Grüningen Castle, childhood home of Conrad. The church steeple rises behind the house.

larly, each generation had at least one—sometimes more—representatives in the Zürich city Council, starting with Lütold. Several female Grebels became nuns in the convent in Zürich, which was a wealthy land-owning convent. The Grebels were merchants and manufacturers, with part of the family engaged in an iron business and another Grebel being a papermaker. Grebels had also served as burgomasters, imperial bailiffs, magistrates, representatives of Zürich at the meetings of the Swiss Confederacy, and soldiers participating in Switzerland's major wars. One Grebel was even knighted for making a pilgrimage to the Holy Land.

It seemed position and prestige ran in the family blood.

Junker[3] Jacob Grebel (c. 1460-1526), Conrad Grebel's father, was one of the most influential of the Grebels. Jacob inherited his father's iron business and had a position in the patrician guild of the city. In 1494, he was elected to the Zürich Council

---

3   In modern Swiss usage, this title has been changed to "von" in front of the last name, as Jacob von Grebel.

of 200,[4] and in 1512 he was elected to the Inner or Small Council. He was somewhat wealthy, as he owned three or four houses. In 1499, the Council appointed him to serve a six-year term as magistrate in the township of Grüningen. This township was just east of Zürich and was one of the largest in the canton. The town of Grüningen itself, however, was a small town, and Jacob probably lived in the castle in the town in his boyhood years.

> **Junker Jacob?**
>
> *Yes, Conrad's father Jacob was a junker! But even though he was in the iron business, he was not a scrap iron dealer. A "junker" is a lower level nobility, a German word that originally meant "young lord."*

Conrad was one of six children born to Jacob and Dorothea (Fries) Grebel. He had four sisters, Barbara, Euphrosine, Martha, and the youngest of the family, Dorothy. He also had one brother, Andreas. Euphrosine became a nun in the convent in Zürich.

The dates of birth of the Grebel children are not known, except for Dorothy's. Conrad's birth year has been estimated at 1498. At the age of seven or eight, Conrad would probably have attended Latin school, as the custom was at the time. He probably learned in the Latin school hosted in the Grossmünster, Zürich's largest cathedral. After a minimum of six years of Latin school, Conrad would have been qualified for enrollment in a University.

University of Basel

In October 1514, Conrad left the canton of Zürich to begin his university education. He was enrolled in the University of Basel (another Swiss city) for the winter semester.

---

4   The "Council of 200" was Zürich's "Large Council," which actually had 212 members.

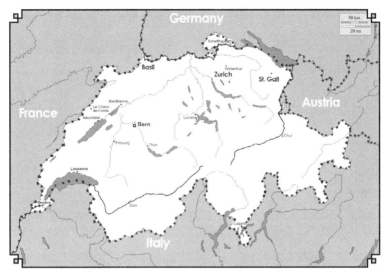

Conrad's first university experience was in Basel,
about 45 miles northwest of Zürich.

While studying at the University of Basel, Conrad Grebel joined the bursa of an independent humanist scholar by the name of Heinrich Loriti (1488-1563), a.k.a. Glarean (after his home in Glarus). A bursa was the name for the houses in which the university students lived. Each bursa housed about fifteen students, who were under the supervision of a professor or an independent scholar (such as Glarean), but who had to be approved by the University. This was a way for the bursa supervisors to get a little extra money, as the students would pay them for providing bed and board. In Glarean's case, it allowed him to continue his own studies while still providing for his living. For the students, this arrangement reduced their expenses and provided them with additional instruction and discipline.

During his stay with Glarean in Basel, Conrad became a good friend of Glarean. Also staying in Glarean's bursa were several other students—Valentin and Peter Tschudi and Johann Leopold Grebel (Conrad's second cousin).

While Glarean was a capable and talented teacher, he was a unique personality. He found it hard to fit in with other

Zürich today. The city in Conrad's time was only about one inch in

diameter on this aerial view, where the Limmat River leaves Lake Zürich.

people, and was given to rapidly changing moods and occasional strange behavior—such as the time he felt he was not being given enough recognition among the professors, so he rode on horseback into a hall where a scholarly disputation was in progress, refusing to leave until the assembly had been dismissed.

Vienna

At the end of the winter semester in 1515, Glarean closed his Basel bursa and left for Italy to study there. Four of his students, including Conrad Grebel, made plans for study in Vienna, Austria. A famous professor, Joachim von Watt, a.k.a. Vadian (1484-1551), from St. Gall (another Swiss canton) was there at Vienna. Ulrich Zwingli, a learned Roman Catholic priest in Glarus, was encouraging Swiss students to go to Vienna. And so they went. On July 4, 1515, Conrad Grebel and three of his fellow-students surrendered their Zürich citizenship, a requirement for attending a foreign university. They set off for Vienna and enrolled in the summer semester. Conrad's father Jacob had secured for him a four-year stipend (scholarship) from the emperor to study in Vienna.

Having arrived in Vienna, the students from Switzerland—including Grebel—may have lived in the bursa run by Vadian. Conrad in particular became quite close to this famous professor, beginning a friendship which would last nearly to the end of Conrad's life. On February 28, 1517, Vadian wrote a letter to Grebel presenting a vision for Grebel's education and how true eloquence and knowledge should both be attained. He printed this letter in a book which he published, presumably about 1517.

In September 1517, Conrad wrote to Ulrich Zwingli, who was now in Einsiedeln in Switzerland. Zwingli had written to Conrad and his second cousin, Johann Leopold. Zwingli

Joachim von Watt, who took the Latin name Vadian, was an eminent scholar who became Conrad's teacher, brother-in-law, and close friend.

often wrote personal letters of encouragement to young Swiss students, many of whom looked up to him as a role model. The cousins were jubilant over receiving a letter from Zwingli, and Conrad wrote back on behalf of both of them. He wrote about his life as a student in Vienna:

> I am studying under Vadian, a man singularly worthy of every honor, by whom, and this I must confess, I am esteemed as a brother, while he himself is loved, cherished, and revered by me as if he were a most devoted father. . . . I would still prefer to be enrolled among the French students of Glarean. . . . having come to the conclusion that he is the preeminent teacher—I pay him the highest honor that is due and give him the garland appropriate to his fame—for he faithfully fulfills all the responsibilities of a learned, good, and true teacher. I felt the lack of these in Vadian, and I hope you will not mind my saying it—not that he was negligent, nor that he was lacking in ability, but that as a candidate in medicine he naturally is caught, so to speak. . . . Engrossed in many

The Grebel house on Neumarkt street in Zürich. On the opposite page is the engraving seen in the lower left.

projects, he is writing a commentary on *Pomponius Mela*,[5] with prolific annotations, to be published in Vienna.[6]

In May, 1518, Vadian's edition of Pomponius Mela was published, complete with an open letter to Conrad at the end of the book. Vadian encouraged Grebel in his pursuit of knowledge. As an additional honor, several of Vadian's students—including Conrad Grebel—contributed poems which were published in the book.

Grebel's life in Vienna included more than study. Vienna at the time was known for its licentiousness and

---

5   Mela was a first-century Latin geographer. Vadian edited and published, with commentary, Mela's surviving work on geography.
6   Conrad Grebel to Ulrich Zwingli, September 8, 1517; from Harder, Leland, editor, *Sources of Swiss Anabaptism*, 1985, Herald Press, p. 56. Used with permission.

*Conrad Grebel, who with Felix Manz founded Anabaptism,
lived in this house from 1508-1514 and 1520-1525.*

drunkenness, particularly among the students. Students also
frequently engaged in brawls, and Grebel was wounded in
a fight. Moreover, in Vienna he contracted a disease which
would plague him for the rest of his life. Historian Harold S.
Bender described the disease from Conrad's letters:

> Grebel repeatedly speaks of his illness. Soon after his
> return from Vienna in 1518 he was compelled to visit
> the thermal baths at Baden in the endeavor to heal a
> virulent abscess on his back, but to no avail. The abscess
> became so serious that for a time he could not write.
> On January 29, 1519, he wrote from Paris that he was
> suffering in his feet not less than had already been the
> case in Vienna. He remarks in this letter that his feet
> pained him because they were pinched by the winter's

To stipend or not to stipend?

Jacob Grebel sought and obtained a stipend for Conrad so he could have a university education. A stipend was similar to a scholarship, although usually given to support the student's living costs while studying abroad.

The issue was a thorny one in Zürich in Conrad's day. Some felt it was a way for foreign governments to stick their fingers into another kingdom's matters. Many Swiss people felt that Jacob Grebel was accepting illegal bribes. Jacob ultimately paid dearly for his decision to take a stipend from a foreign government, as we shall see at the end of this story.

cold, "and deservedly so, since oft have I consorted with females carnally," but counts the disease a curable one, at least if Vadian will help him by good medical advice. On April 25, 1521, his feet were so inflamed that he could not travel. In July, 1521, he reported that the illness often attacked the joints of both hands and feet at the same time. November 2, 1521, he requested Vadian again for counsel regarding the use of the baths as a curative measure. As late as May, 1525, he wrote to Castelberger that he had great difficulty in walking on account of his feet. What the illness was can no longer be determined with accuracy. It may have been rheumatism, or something more serious. L. von Muralt reports that a Zurich physician, Dr. B. Milt, to whom he submitted the evidence, diagnosed the trouble as chilblain.[7] At any rate it was something which started in Vienna and plagued him to the end of his life.[8]

---

7   This is a painful swelling on feet or hands from exposure to cold.

8   Harold S. Bender, *Conrad Grebel 1498-1526: Founder of the Swiss Brethren*, 1950, Mennonite Historical Society, p. 233. Parenthetical references omitted from quote.

This scene, the earliest extant painting by the famous portrait painter Hans Holbien the Younger, was part of an advertising signboard for the teacher Oswald Myconius, who became a good friend of Conrad. Note the older students, as well as the rare glimpse of the interior of a Zürich building in 1516.

The fight in which he had engaged was to cost Grebel the final year of his intended course of study in Vienna. Grebel later explained to Zwingli:

> I was wounded, but in truth had already recovered. A friend, who was not a friend, reported this to my father before my return, and he lied saying that I was worse than I was. Worried because of this, father ordered me to return from Vienna at once, going along with Vadian. So I returned, but not before the family of Vadian had graciously entertained me at St. Gallen.[9]

In addition to having been summoned home by his father, it is possible that Grebel's return home was partly due to the spreading of the plague in Vienna, as Vadian also suddenly returned to Switzerland at the same time. Another possible reason for Grebel's return is that his father seems to have been able to secure a French stipend for his son to study in Paris.

---

9   Conrad Grebel to Ulrich Zwingli, July 31, 1518; from Harder, Leland, editor, *Sources of Swiss Anabaptism*, 1985, Herald Press, p. 64. Used with permission.

Pontius Pilate's gravesite?

Did you ever wonder what happened to Pontius Pilate? Where was he buried? Well, to be honest, no one really knows. Stories floated around for centuries, but the stories did not always match. Some say he died in prison at Rome, while other stories place his death in foreign lands. Obviously, at least some of the stories, if not all of them, were incorrect.

One popular myth was that when Pilate died, his body was thrown into the Tiber River that flows through Rome. The evil spirits in the river threw a fit and caused the river to back up and cause terrible floods. The body was then pulled from the Tiber and dumped in the Rhone River, which drains Lake Geneva in western Switzerland and flows south through France. When the Rhone acted similarly to the Tiber, the body was then taken to Switzerland and dumped in a lake. Yet another version of the story is that Pilate was so distraught after his dealings with Jesus that he wandered to Mount Pilatus (6,982 feet elevation, approximately 30 miles southeast of Zürich) in Switzerland and committed suicide by drowning himself in a small lake on the mountain.

The truth is that nobody knows what really happened to Pontius Pilate. However, the truth is also that the local people—at least some of them—around Mount Pilatus believed that Pilate was indeed buried in a small lake high up on the mountain. It was said that on every Good Friday he came out of the lake and washed his hands once again of the blood of Jesus.

The story of terrible storms originating from human disturbance of the lake is what drew Conrad, Vadian, and some friends to investigate. Perhaps it was more of an adventure for a group of young men than a bona-fide "science experiment." None the less, Vadian has earned the reputation of being the first man recorded to have reached the peak of the mountain. Most likely some unknown locals had already been there, but Vadian got the "honor."

Mount Pilatus is said to have been named after Pontius Pilate, but the name may simply be a corruption of Pileatus, meaning "cloud-topped." In 1585, the priest at nearby Luzern took on the challenge of the lake's hauntedness. He and a group of men threw stones into the lake, waded into it, and basically did all they could to test the myth. Nothing happened. A few years later, a channel was dug so as to drain the lake, to quell any further fears. Only in 1980 did the channel get refilled and the lake formed anew. It is really not much of a lake, less than one acre in size and nameless on most maps.

Today Mount Pilatus is a huge tourist attraction, with the world's steepest cog railway going up one side and a cable car up the other. A large hotel sits near the peak. The photo above is taken from the top, looking northeast over Lake Luzern, with the city on the left. The story of Pilate's burial in the lake is now considered but another medieval myth alongside similar ones of fire-breathing dragons that also dwelt on the cloud-topped mountain.

Bathing at Baden

Yes, that is what happened at Baden. The German word "baden" means just that ... baths! In the Swiss town of that name, located about 12 miles west of Zürich (there is a German town with the same name), 117° F water flows from several springs. From early Roman times, the springs were used for medicinal purposes, although they did not have the reputation of miraculous healing. Most likely it was considered a luxury to soak in good hot water on a cold Swiss winter day. So when Conrad went to Baden, he often went to take a bath!

A Scientific Expedition

While in Zürich, Grebel became friends with Oswald Myconius, one of the teachers at the Grossmünster school. Vadian came to visit the Grebels in Zürich, and soon after, the three men left for the Swiss town of Luzern. The purpose of the expedition was to ascend "Mt. Pilatus," a mountain near Luzern. According to local lore, the lake (more like a swamp) near the summit of the mountain was the final resting place of the remains of Pontius Pilate, and whenever a human hand maliciously threw any item into the swamp, a great tempest would arise and the whole region would be flooded. This rumor held such a grip on the minds of the locals that anyone who wanted to climb the mountain had to get a license from the city authorities. Vadian and his friends—along with the local pastor, John Zimmerman—got the necessary license from the authorities and went about their mountain climb, said to be the first scientific mountain ascent. The purpose of the climb was to test the legend by throwing something into the lake. Partway up the mountain, when their horses were tired, they let the horses rest in a pasture and hired a shepherd to guide them the rest of the way up the mountain to the lake.

The shepherd was quite nervous at the prospect that these scientific visitors would endanger his life, and tried to get them to swear an oath that they would not throw anything into the lake. He kept up his frightened talk all the way up to the lake, which was surrounded by forest. By the time they arrived, Vadian had concluded that he would not be able to test the legend after all without causing great panic. So the legend remained untested and the locals would continue to repeat it.

After climbing Mt. Pilatus with Vadian, Conrad went to the Swiss city of Baden, where his married sister Barbara lived, to try to alleviate his illness by partaking in the medicinal baths for which the city was noted. However, as soon as he got home to Zürich, a sore in the middle of his back became so bad that he could hardly do anything—not even write.

In September, 1518, Conrad wrote to Vadian, reporting that he was headed to Paris to study with Glarean. He had received a pension from the king of France to do so. Furthermore, he helped Vadian with something they had discussed before—namely, arranging for Vadian to possibly marry Martha, Conrad's sister. Conrad was eager to have his best friend be his brother-in-law.

Paris

Paris, a city with a population of 250,000 people, was the home of the king of France, and of a renowned university. It was a center of scholarship and learning. Having arrived with three other Zürichers in Paris, Conrad joined Glarean's bursa and began attending his lectures.

But Conrad was not to have a long, peaceful period of study in Paris. Rather, his time in France was marked by constant trouble and calamity—and complaining letters to his friends in Switzerland.

Soon after arriving at Paris, Conrad wrote a letter to Vadian, in which he called Glarean "the best of men." Glarean, however, was to have a frustrating time in Paris. He had failed to secure

These guys killed 1/2 of Europe!

Yes, those tiny bacteria, seen only under a microscope, are now considered the agent that left Europe with half of its population dead. But that is only part of the story!

In A.D. 541-542, it was reported that 10,000 people were dying every day in Constantinople. Eventually, 40% of the population of the city died. As the plague spread into surrounding areas, one fourth of the people in east Asia died. But it didn't stop there. In 588, the disease hit France and spread throughout Europe. Called the Plague of Justinian (emperor at the time the plague first hit), scholars estimate that up to 50% of the European population succumbed to the tiny invaders in the next two centuries.

The next major invasion hit in 1347 A.D. This pandemic is what is commonly known as "The Black Death." Although it cannot be proven, it may be a case of biological warfare that started its dark task of killing millions of Europeans once again. Merchants from Genoa (now part of Italy) had bought the port of Caffa (modern Feodosia) in the Crimea and were operating a monopolous trade in the Black Sea. Mongol invaders tried to take over the city, but were losing multitudes of their army to the plague. They then catapulted the dead bodies over the city wall—and the disease started spreading inside the city. Fleeing the city, the residents may have then carried the disease back to ports in Italy, from whence it spread all over Europe during the next four years. But it needs to be reiterated that this can only be conjectured through a reconstruction of events, and is not universally recognized as the original source of The Black Death in Europe.

It is very difficult for us today to realize the fear and dread of plague outbreaks. We read of millions of deaths, people going into panic, and some small towns where 100% of the people died. Then we turn the page, grab a drink of water, and continue reading.

Imagine now, that your neighbors are dying faster than anyone can bury them. The governments are sending out flyers claiming that the air is bad because of the alignment of three stars. Others are saying it is the Jews' fault,

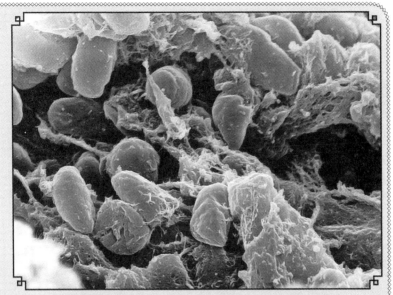

Yersinia pestis *bacteria under a microscope.*

and are annihilating entire towns of Jews. Yet others are blaming the Gypsies. Some are saying it is a punishment from God for the sins of the people.

No one suspects the lowly rats. Yet, it is not even the rats which are killing the people. In fact, the rats are dying from it as well! In China (where the bacteria are thought to have originated), people had recognized that the mass dying of rats was usually a sign that the plague was soon to follow.

So was it the fault of the fleas on the rats? No, they were also dying by multitudes, but no one took the time to examine them. The fleas would ingest some of the bacteria, which would multiply in their guts, causing a blockage. The fleas would then try to drink more blood, but had to regurgitate it into a host animal. The flea would keep trying to drink more blood, but could not keep it down because of the blockage in its guts. Hungry, it would drink, then vomit. Eventually the flea would die of hunger.

By these means, fleas and rats and other rodents, the bacteria spread from town to town. When the bacteria entered a human (via a flea bite, infection from a cough, etc), three manifestations could happen.

　1. The Bubonic form: The bacteria would infect the lymph nodes, often in the groin area, causing them to swell to the size of an egg or even an apple.

　2. The Septicemic form: If the bacteria entered the blood stream, they caused internal bleeding. This bleeding produced black spots under the skin

and eventually death in the tissue, which may cause the tissue to turn black. This may have been why the plague was called The Black Death.

3. The Pneumonic form: If the lungs got infected, coughing and spitting of blood was common. This form spread rapidly by coughing, and death was quick to follow infection.

The death rate for the first two forms was about 80-90%. The last form was close to 100%. From the time of infection—which may not be noticed immediately—to death was usually just days. Thus the bacteria spread through Europe again, beginning in 1347. For the next several centuries reoccurences would pop up in various cities. Europe again lost 1/3 of its population. China lost half, and parts of Africa lost up to 1/8.

As you continue reading the story of Conrad Grebel, you will encounter the plague in various parts of his life. In fact, Conrad himself was a victim of the *Yersinia pestis* hordes. Ulrich Zwingli got it and survived.

One simply cannot "feel" the story of Conrad without adding in the dimension of The Black Death and its grip of terror over the world in his days. As you continue reading about Conrad, keep in mind that a foreboding shadow is constantly moving over the scene, first here, then there. Always hovering, always threatening. Always moving silently hither and yon, but never leaving the stage.

Interestingly, the exact *Yersinia pestis* strain that caused The Black Death seems to have disappeared in our day. Other strains still plague the world, including an estimated 10-15 people annually in the USA.

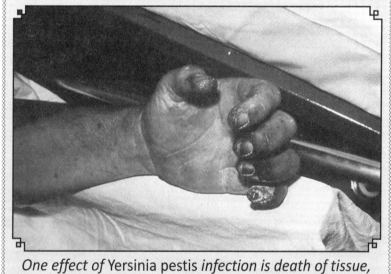

One effect of Yersinia pestis *infection is death of tissue,*
causing it to turn black, as in this photo.

the vacant position of professor of poetry at the University of Paris. However, he did receive the pay for the job with no obligation to lecture any more than he wished to. Thus, he had written to the famous humanist scholar Erasmus, "now I stay at home, making a little music to my pupils and abandoned to idleness. I enjoy myself with my beloved Horace and laugh with Democritus at the folly of the world."[10]

Conrad was assigned to a room in Glarean's bursa with three other students. Unfortunately for Conrad, the room lacked a fireplace, and he suffered much from his recurring illness due to the cold. "The winter froze my limbs which are impatient with the cold," he later told Vadian.[11] He asked Glarean for permission to switch rooms, for which Glarean called him soft and opposed the plan. Glarean had promised to move the bursa to a more spacious location, but did not deliver on the promise until a few of his students annoyed the landlord, who ordered Glarean out of the house. They moved to another location, and Conrad chose a room with a fireplace and a study—which Glarean allowed him to use only after some grumbling. With the assistance of some of his friends, Conrad installed a stove in the study, but it did not work very well. It smoked and annoyed the others, who threatened to smash it. The matter caused significant contention between Conrad and Glarean, and it became obvious to Grebel that he was going to have to leave the bursa before the contention came to blows.

The breaking point came when some soldiers were guests in Glarean's bursa for an evening. It was an occasion of revelry, and Conrad became drunk. Disgusted at the way his student was acting and speaking, Glarean ordered Conrad to be taken away to his room. After he sobered, Conrad knew that his behavior was extremely disgusting to Glarean. Glarean nursed

---

10   As cited in Harder, Leland, editor, *Sources of Swiss Anabaptism*, 1985, Herald Press, p. 76. Used with permission. Horace and Democritus were ancient authors.
11   Conrad Grebel to Vadian, January 29, 1519; from Harder, Leland, editor, *Sources of Swiss Anabaptism*, 1985, Herald Press, p. 77. Used with permission.

a grudge, yet did not reprove Conrad. Soon after, another student who got drunk was given kinder treatment by Glarean. A few days after Conrad's offense, Glarean finally gave a kind reproof, and Conrad asked for forgiveness. Nevertheless, he knew that Glarean would continue to hold a grudge. In anger, Conrad swore a solemn oath that he would leave the bursa as soon as possible.

With a few of his friends, Conrad found a house which had steam heating and made plans to move. Although Glarean was extremely opposed to the idea of Conrad's leaving, Conrad insisted, and moved out on January 1, 1519.

Yet Conrad's troubles were far from over, and his move would not solve his difficulties. Not long after moving, Conrad wrote a letter to Vadian, recounting his grievances in detail. Vadian did not write back for months, and when he did, he reproved his former student. In the meantime, Oswald Myconius—another friend of Grebel's, to whom he wrote about the incident but with much less detail than he had written to Vadian—continued a loyal friend and helper for Conrad.

On May 1, 1519, another calamity was to befall young Conrad. While out with a group of other Swiss students in the city of Paris, they were apparently attacked by bandits. In self-defense, the Swiss students killed two of the bandits. The incident nearly cost Conrad his life at the hands of the law, and it nearly cost Glarean his bursa. The remaining details, as revealed by the letters of the concerned parties, are sketchy. Needless to say, when Jacob Grebel and Vadian heard of the situation, they were much displeased with Conrad.

Conrad's studies were to be still further disrupted by the plague. In the summer of 1519, the plague raged through the city of Paris, and Conrad fled with three of his friends ten miles away from the city. Here they remained until January 1520. In the meantime, about 30,000 people died in Paris. At the same time, the plague was also raging in Switzerland. Ulrich

Zwingli was sick with it, although he recovered. Vadian took a long holiday from St. Gall to avoid it.

In October, 1519, Conrad finally heard again from Vadian. He had written a letter telling Conrad that he had married Martha Grebel, Conrad's sister. Conrad was wildly happy, until he learned that his father had not sent him any money to come home to attend the wedding. He was incredibly upset about that. He learned from Vadian that his father was very displeased with him, a fact that did not surprise him.

Furthermore, Conrad's monetary funds were dangerously low. His father did not faithfully send on to his son the scholarships which he had received from the French king.[12] Lack of money would trouble Conrad the rest of his life.

Finally, in January 1520, Conrad moved back to the city of Paris. Soon after, he received a letter from his father which had been written in September of the previous year. On the same day, he received a negative letter from Vadian, and a letter from Oswald Myconius informing him about the state of affairs in Conrad's parents' home.

Out of money, Conrad had asked his father for more. His father obliged, entrusting the money to the messenger with the letter. The letter arrived, but the money did not. The money had been "lost." In the letter, Jacob Grebel ordered his son to return home and to abandon the bad companions who had nearly cost him his life. He was afraid that Conrad had acted dishonorably and wasted his time and money. While Conrad denied these charges, he could not return home even if he had wanted to—he had no money. Through Myconius, Conrad's mother advised him to remain in Paris until his father's anger had cooled. In the meantime, because of his financial straits, Conrad returned to Glarean's bursa, although not as a regular student member.

---

12   Conrad only ever received 1/3 of the scholarship from the French king; his father kept the rest.

In his letter to Myconius in which he tells about his financial woes, Conrad waxes eloquent about his worries regarding the scholarships he had received. He wished that his father had taught him better monetary responsibility—to live on what he had earned, even if that was not much, rather than taking from others for extravagant living. He feared a day of reckoning was coming for his father and himself for taking this money; his patriotic friends were not pleased with his father's and his actions regarding the scholarships. Conrad—patriotic himself—was greatly troubled with this, even though he hoped that there was nothing illegal about taking the scholarships. His worries were to prove prophetic.

In July, 1520, Conrad at last left Paris for home in Zürich. Apparently, his father had finally given him the necessary funds, and Conrad came home—his student days over.

Back in Zürich

Conrad finally arrived home, after years of study, "fun," trouble, disease, disappointment, and sin. He described his homecoming in a letter to Vadian, who was still turning a cold shoulder toward his brother-in-law:

> I came to my own home, which is not my own, to friends not my friends, to my appeased parents, both of whom received me in a human way, the one with a father's scorn, the other with a mother's tears. I imitated the two of them in turn. As did the parents, so did the son.[13]

Adding to Conrad's melancholy was the fact that just before his arrival in Zürich, his sister Euphrosine—a nun at the Oetenbach convent in Zürich—had died. Conrad was grieved and prayed that she would be rewarded for her pure life.

---

13   Conrad Grebel to Vadian, July 13, 1520; from Harder, Leland, editor, *Sources of Swiss Anabaptism*, 1985, Herald Press, p. 109. Used with permission.

Prayers, indulgences, and purgatory

Conrad, like most Catholics, offered prayers for his deceased relatives. In Catholicism, prayers are offered for the dead because of the belief in purgatory. The doctrine of purgatory states that all sins will have *temporal* consequences while on earth, even though the *eternal* consequence has been pardoned by Christ. If the *temporal* consequence is not fully played out while on earth—in the vast majority of cases that does not happen, according to Catholic teaching—then the soul must suffer more *temporal* consequences in purgatory before going to heaven. A person can reduce these *temporal* consequences by doing good deeds as a sign of repentance, but few people get that completely accomplished while living.

It is a common misconception by non-Catholics that the buying of indulgences was a way to buy *eternal* forgiveness. Indulgences were a way to help reduce the time in purgatory, because the indulgence was really supposed to be a good work that showed the purchaser was truly repentant of his past sinful life and was now going to spend his life living righteously. For example, if someone spent $100 on an indulgence, it was supposed to be seen as a $100 donation to the Church so the Church could use the money for doing good, like helping the poor, or building a chapel. So, according to Catholic doctrine, that $100 donation would then take away from the buyer's time in purgatory, since it showed repentance in the buyer: the buyer was turning from practicing sin to practicing charity. If the purchaser wanted, he could even have this "credit" applied to a deceased friend's "account."

Time in purgatory could also be reduced by prayers and fasting. Again, this was *supposed* to be a sign of penitence and change of life, not a mere "buying" of forgiveness. However, in medieval days, the line seems to have been pretty blurry between official doctrine and what was preached in the pulpits and by the indulgence sellers.

Prayers for the dead were made to help relatives and friends pass through purgatory faster. Because, according to Catholic doctrine, Christians everywhere are always united in one body - those living and those dead - the faithful on earth can help the faithful in purgatory, and the saints in heaven can help the faithful on earth by intercession. The saints in heaven were petitioned by the faithful still on earth to help pray, and prayers were made for the faithful still suffering in purgatory so they could pass the *temporal* consequences of their sins faster.

Having returned home, for the next months, Conrad did
— nothing. Almost nothing, that is. He studied Greek some,
but beyond that, his scholarly pursuits had come to a halt.

The Reformation Begins

Throughout his student years, Grebel did not seem to be a
very religious person. He mentioned God, Christ, and going
to church in his letters, but he was more likely to allude to
Greek mythology or swear by the Greek and Roman deities.
The scholarly pursuit of eloquence interested him far more
than religion. However, whether Conrad cared about it or
not, the religious scene in Europe was being changed pro-
foundly.

Beginning about 1517, Martin Luther began preaching
church reform in Germany, stirring up intense controversy.
His reformation spread far and wide. In 1519, Zwingli was
called to Zürich to be the people's priest at the Grossmünster
chapel.[14] On assuming this job, Zwingli promised to preach
nothing but the Gospel—that is, he would preach expository
messages directly from the Scriptures rather than following
the official listing of passages to be read. Furthermore, he
would not necessarily interpret them in accordance with the
interpretations of former, well-respected teachers and theolo-
gians. Thus Zwingli's reforming labors in Zürich began as he
started with the Gospel of Matthew. After having recovered
from his bout with the plague, Zwingli's personal sense of
mission in the reformation heightened, and he pursued it with
a new zeal and consecration.

Like Luther, Zwingli had his critics and his followers. Oswald
Myconius, Grebel's close friend, was one of Zwingli's supporters. A schoolmaster in the town of Luzern, Myconius spread
the doctrines of Zwingli's reformation and encountered great
opposition from the Roman Catholic populace. On July 24,

14   The duty of the people's priest was preaching more than dispensing the
sacraments.

1520, Zwingli wrote a letter of encouragement to Myconius, in which he said: "I believe that as the church was brought forth in blood, so it can be renewed through blood and in no other way."[15] Zwingli's attitude of readiness for persecution and martyrdom at this point in the reformation was to contrast greatly with his actions later.

Grebel's Inactivity and Indecision

While all of the excitement of the Reformation was stirring around him, Conrad Grebel took little part. Rather, he planned a trip to visit Vadian and his sister Martha in St. Gall. His family was eager for him to go, and Vadian invited him more than once. Conrad, however, stayed at home, waiting for his books to arrive from Paris—because with his books was to arrive some "other things which my father must not see," he told Vadian.[16] He told this to Vadian in late July, and his books did not arrive until September. He read a few Reformation tracts, including one "on not going to war" by his friend, Oswald Myconius. Grebel said that this tract, "by reason of its truth deserves to become a classic."[17] In September, his books finally arrived from Paris, but he still had to stay at home. His father was away from home when they arrived, and business was pressing at the family iron shop. Since the foreman was not yet experienced, Conrad had to stay in Zürich to help out—so the visit to Vadian was delayed further.

---

15   Ulrich Zwingli to Oswald Myconius, July 24, 1520; from Harder, Leland, editor, *Sources of Swiss Anabaptism*, 1985, Herald Press, p. 114. Used with permission.
16   Conrad Grebel to Vadian, July 29, 1520; from Harder, Leland, editor, *Sources of Swiss Anabaptism*, 1985, Herald Press, p. 117. Used with permission.
17   Conrad Grebel to Vadian, August 3, 1520; from Harder, Leland, editor, *Sources of Swiss Anabaptism*, 1985, Herald Press, p. 119. Used with permission.

The Virgin Mary: Intercessor?

Conrad Grebel made a vow to Mary, something quite normal for a medieval Catholic. As in the case of prayers for the dead (see page 27), official Church dogma and what was taught and practiced in the streets were not exactly in sync.

Since Catholic doctrine states that believers who died are living in heaven but are still united in spirit with believers living on earth, asking Mary (or another Saint) to intercede for you was considered no different than asking your pastor or friend to pray for you. Official Catholic dogma does not teach that Mary is equal to Christ, but only that Mary—being Jesus' Mother and therefore extra special to Him—has a special relationship with Him. So if you want someone to intercede for you, why not ask the person most special to Jesus—in Catholics' eyes, Mary?

Despite clear Church dogma stating that Mary was *not* equal to Christ (and despite the fact that Mary being Mediatrix and Co-Redeemer is not official Catholic dogma) many Catholics have—for centuries now—pushed *honoring* her (veneration) into *worshipping* her.

To honor Mary for her devotion to God and for being chosen as the mother of Jesus is not wrong, just like we today may honor Conrad Grebel for his devotion to God. But when honoring someone turns into worshipping that person, we have stepped into idolatry! We are called to honor all men, but to worship God alone!

Finally, in October, Conrad was able to make the long-awaited trip to St. Gall. He had gone with his father to see a representative from the pope who was giving out scholarships. The pope's representative offered to give Conrad a scholarship to the University of Pisa in Italy. Jacob Grebel was pleased at the prospect of Conrad spending two years studying under papal support, and asked Vadian to advise his son.

After returning to Zürich from his brief visit to St. Gall, Grebel decided to go to Italy to take advantage of the offered scholarship. First he made a brief trip to the Swiss town of

Einsiedeln (a resort where Zwingli had been pastor before coming to Zürich) to fulfill a vow he had made to the "Blessed Virgin Mary." He then planned to prepare for the trip to Italy.

Yet the month of December found him still in the city of Zürich—"now at last preparing for the journey, to make my way to Pisa," he told Vadian.[18] (He had said something similar over a month before.) Conrad was to remain for some time in a state of indecision over whether to leave for Pisa or not.

Vadian, in the meantime, was working towards publishing a second edition of his *Commentary on Pomponius Mela*. Conrad had the honor of writing the introduction to the work.

The new year came, and in the month of February, Conrad was still at home—suffering from his disease and wretched from inactivity and indecision. He wrote to Vadian:

> While I am stuck here, fit for nothing, disgracefully wasting my time under the pretense of literary study which I have not pretended since your departure, while, I say, I am stuck here fixed to these walls, fixed to others also, the desire to go to Basel and live there has grown on me. There are reasons it has grown on me, which this sheet, if it could encompass them all, should not or would not want to encompass. I wish I could tell you personally how it happened that the aversion for Italy came over me, how I came to know it. How bad is the reputation of father and son because of my stipend [scholarship], my uncles impress upon me daily. So it happens that I could not feel much joy in accepting this papal wealth.[19]

Besides Conrad's aversion to accepting another foreign scholarship, he had another reason for the new desire to go to the Swiss city of Basel, which he was to reveal to his friends and family only slowly and as secretly as possible.

---

18   Conrad Grebel to Vadian, December 8, 1520; from Harder, Leland, editor, *Sources of Swiss Anabaptism*, 1985, Herald Press, p. 130. Used with permission.
19   Conrad Grebel to Vadian, February 1, 1521; Harder, Leland, editor, *Sources of Swiss Anabaptism*, 1985, Herald Press, p. 136. Used with permission.

In the meantime, the pope's representative visited Conrad and offered to pay his travel expenses to Pisa. The scholarship itself, however, would not be paid until Conrad had actually arrived at the city. The pope's man left and Conrad stayed in Zürich.

In late April, 1521, Conrad's mother fell seriously ill, and Vadian—who was a physician—hurried to Zürich with his wife. He returned in May, leaving Martha behind for a while to be with her recovering mother.

Conrad's *Holokosmos*

The reason why Conrad wanted to go to Basel was a girl—a girl by the name of Barbara.[20] Conrad and Barbara had "fallen in love" and Conrad would later call her his *Holokosmos*, "whole world." While originally a secret—especially from his parents—Conrad's aunt Agatha got Conrad to reveal his secret to her, and besought him not to conceal the matter from the nuns in the Oetenbach convent in Zürich.[21] She approved of his plan to make his escape to Basel, where he could be together with Barbara. During the summer of 1521, Conrad wrote to Vadian about the situation and told him that he was waiting for his father to recover from a kidney stone before he tried to leave Zürich. As the summer wore on and he continued to long to depart for Basel with Barbara, his older sister (also named Barbara) was let in on the secret and she agreed to be an intermediary between Conrad and his parents when the time came. Conrad sent Barbara to Basel ahead of him at his own expense and was ready to follow her as soon as possible.

---

20   Her last name is unknown.
21   Why Conrad would need to tell the nuns about the situation is unknown. Some historians have speculated that Barbara was a nun in the convent, or at least that she had been living in the convent (without being a member of the order). This would also explain why Conrad's parents were so bitterly opposed to the marriage. This explanation, however, is quite speculative.

Vadian apparently approved of Conrad's plan to go to Basel, and in July wrote asking why he was still in Zürich. Conrad replied, informing Vadian of his father's opposition to the plan and how they had argued over his departure. He disliked staying at home very much—even aside from missing Barbara—and wanted to leave. He was so distraught that he could not sleep at night, and his disease attacked the joints in his hands and feet, giving him much misery.

In August, 1521, Conrad was finally able to get away from Zürich and arrive at Basel, where he could be together with Barbara, his *Holokosmos*. He had used some of the money which the pope's representative had given him to get to Basel. Although he was happy for the moment, he was to find out that romance and fornication could not solve all of his problems nor give lasting peace and joy.

While Barbara stayed in another room in the city, Grebel stayed with the printer Andreas Cratander, who was at the time printing the second edition of Vadian's *Pomponius Mela*. Grebel started working for Cratander, who was thrilled to have the young scholar in his shop. In September, Cratander left for Frankfort to sell books at the book fair, leaving Conrad to himself for a while. Conrad wrote to Vadian of the expense in paying for separate lodgings for himself and Barbara, and considered having one lodging—although it is not known if he carried out this plan. Humorously, after writing of all his financial difficulties to Vadian, he asked his brother-in-law to find some red silk for a fancy cloak and send it to him without his parents' knowledge, promising to repay him in the following year.

Back in Zürich

After spending two months in Basel working at the print shop and secretly being with Barbara, Conrad moved back to Zürich with Barbara. He had been summoned home by

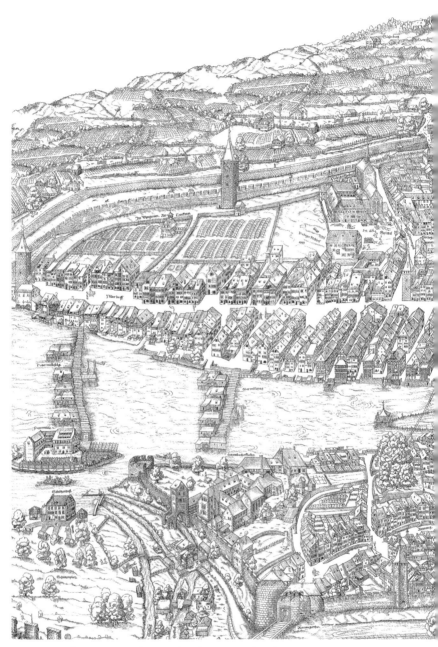

Another view of Zürich, this time looking east in 1576.

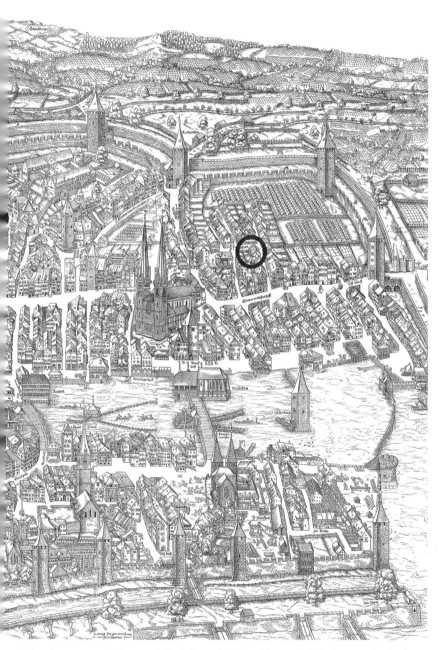

The houses of Conrad (left) and Felix Manz (right) are circled.

his parents on account of his poor health; they wanted him to take medicinal baths. Additionally, Conrad's brother Andreas had died while Conrad was in Basel. Barbara stayed elsewhere in the city with Conrad's support. Conrad wrote to Vadian:

> I have said a final farewell to roaming about. I prefer to be in my native land, whether well or rather miserable. In my private study, if it will please the gods, I shall read something from Lucian and I shall taste the wit and elegance of the Greek epigrams. This will probably be my last exercise in the literature of both languages. I have been most unsuccessful in devoting diligent attention to my studious inclinations, troubled by intolerable calamities; and this is the reason that I am always immediately torn from the unlucky course of studies, so often thwarted. I have loved (them) and I do love (them), you know how![22]

In poor health, with his *Holokosmos* still a secret from his parents, not able to complete the studies he had loved—Conrad Grebel was back in Zürich, but still not free from his "calamities." Yet he joined a small group of scholars studying the writings of Plato with Ulrich Zwingli. This study group was to be the beginning of a turning point in Conrad Grebel's life.

Marriage

Conrad was finally able to fulfill his desire in regards to Barbara. On February 6, 1522, they were formally married. Conrad had taken the opportunity to do this while his father was away on a week of business. On the same day, Conrad wrote to Vadian:

---

22   Conrad Grebel to Vadian, November 2, 1521; from Harder, Leland, editor, *Sources of Swiss Anabaptism*, 1985, Herald Press, pp. 155-156. Used with permission.

Defining "gospel"

Today we often think of the "gospel" or "good news" in terms of a message that only concerns how a person is saved. However, the term was used differently in the Zwinglian Reformation. Historian Harold Bender explains: "When Zwingli and the people considered themselves to be 'evangelical,' they thought in general of the 'Gospel' as a more or less clear and fixed entity to be found in the Scripture, out of which it would be possible to secure the guidance necessary to meet the needs of the church. As a matter of fact, however, no one had systematically thought through the 'Gospel' and outlined a clear program which was accepted by all. The concept 'Gospel,' as current among the people, covered a multitude of diverse religious and ethical notions, some of which had arisen out of Zwingli's preaching, some of which were derived out of the constantly growing number of popular religious tracts, and some of which were the result of personal study of the Bible." (Bender, *Conrad Grebel*, pp. 89-90).

From this we see that to the people in the 16th century, "the gospel" was the whole message of the Bible, including doctrines and practical applications. Today, "the gospel" has come to mean, for many people, only forgiveness of sins.

I have just now wedded Barbara, mine I hope. I confessed it first to our friend Hans Wirz, and then to Master Doctor Engelhart,[23] and to certain others who promised their intercession when father returns. Mother sheds tears constantly. She is intemperate toward me, no doubt the most unfortunate of all men. If father continues to treat

---

23   Both of these men were relatives of the Grebels. Engelhart was the head priest at the Fraumünster cathedral in Zürich.

me in the same way and to behave as she does, you will have seen the last of Conrad in these parts.[24]

After writing this letter, Conrad's pen fell silent for nearly ten months, until November. In that time, he would experience a deep and profound change in his life. His contact with Zwingli would culminate in his own conversion, which is easily noticed in his letters. His wanderings through far-off lands, wasting his life and money in riotous living, would soon be over. He would return to his Heavenly Father with the plea, "Forgive me, Father, for I have sinned."

---

24   Conrad Grebel to Vadian, February 6, 1522; from Harder, Leland, editor, *Sources of Swiss Anabaptism*, 1985, Herald Press, p. 165. Used with permission.

Ulrich Zwingli is remembered in Zürich by this statue portraying him with a Bible in one hand and a sword in the other, an unfortunate but true representation.

2

Reformer's Aide

onrad Grebel had finally attained what he had desired for some time—marriage to his *Holokosmos*, Barbara. His parents still opposed him and he was still low on funds. But his life was about to make a major turn. He was to forsake the way of sin and become an outspoken proponent of the Gospel.

Breaking the Fast

Ulrich Zwingli had preached the reform of the church for some time since his arrival in Zürich in late 1518, but there had been no open break with the Roman Catholic Church as a result of Zwingli's preaching until 1522. Zwingli had gathered around himself several men who supported his teachings, and in March, 1522, on Ash Wednesday, they were ready to put into practice the reform and the break with Catholic tradition that Zwingli had been encouraging.

It was an evening gathering in the home of Christopher Froschauer. Froschauer was a Bavarian printer who had moved to Zürich and had been given citizenship there two years before.

He was a skilled printer whose work was very valuable to the town—and to the Reformation. In later years, he would become the publisher of the famous Froschauer Bible.

On this particular Ash Wednesday evening in 1522, the workers in Froschauer's shop had been working hard to complete a printing of the epistles of Paul for sale at the Frankfurt book fair. The work of the day done, Froschauer had several Reformation-minded men over for dinner, including Ulrich Zwingli, Leo Jud (Zwingli's right-hand man), and some others whom we will meet again later in our story—Hans Ockenfuss, Claus Hottinger, Heinrich Aberli, and Bartlime Pur. In spite of the established tradition of abstaining from meat during Lent (which begins on Ash Wednesday), his wife fried two sausages, and Froschauer cut them into small pieces and passed them around. Almost everyone (except Zwingli) ate a piece.

It was not long before the stunning violation of tradition became known throughout Zürich. Zwingli defended himself, pointing out that he had not eaten a piece, but he refused to rebuke those who had. The city Council was not pleased, and Froschauer and his men were imprisoned—in spite of the fact that Froschauer claimed that the heavy work load compelled them to take nourishing food.

Less than three weeks after the fast violation, Zwingli preached a sermon in the Grossmünster titled "Concerning the Choice and Freedom of Foods." Zwingli said that the kingdom of God is not food and drink, and since the Bible does not command fasting during Lent, the prohibition should not be tolerated indefinitely. However, it was not good to offend those who did not yet understand this.

The Catholic bishop of Constance, who had jurisdiction over Zürich, tried to get the Zürich council on his side against Zwingli. Zwingli was keen to keep this from happening, and as it turned out, he won a notable victory when the Council of 200 took his side and released the sausage-eaters with the command to go to confession and to abstain from any further

The sausages that fired the Reformation

Two small sausages, fried by a printer's wife, are held by some as the spark that lit the Protestant Reformation in Switzerland. Those little sausages even caused Christoph Froschauer and his friends a bit of jail time.

What's the big deal about a bite of sausage? The "big deal" was that the Catholic Church declared it wrong to eat meat during Lent. Of course, the Bible never talks about Lenten fasting for 40 days before Easter. So, reasoned Zwingli, Froschauer, and others, the church should not force people to fast during those days. If someone voluntarily wanted to abstain from meat during those days, fine. But no one had the authority to enforce a universal fast if the Bible never mentions such a thing, nor contains a principle that would suggest it.

The real issue, of course, was not about eating a piece of pork. The issue was the final authority in church practice. It was the always-lingering question of tradition vs. the Bible.

Zwingli (and the later Anabaptist movement) took the position that church traditions were beneath the authority of the written Scriptures. Traditionalists within the Catholic Church held that the Church and its Tradition held equal, if not greater, authority in establishing doctrine and practice.

Historically, those who strip traditions of their authority usually take one of two options. Option one says that the church does indeed have the authority to establish practice and doctrine, but the established practices and doctrines must be within the authority of the written Word of God.

Option two says the church has no authority to establish practice and doctrine. Each individual makes his/her own decision about practice and doctrine.

The difference is between throwing church authority totally out the door vs. keeping the church's authority based on biblical principles. Those churches which have historically thrown out all tradition and church authority as evil have soon found themselves in a quandary. They find themselves bogged down in the quagmire of individualism, the opposite ditch of traditionalism.

provocative actions. They also approved Zwingli's sermon as Biblically sound teaching, although it would not be put into practice yet.

Grebel's Conversion

In the meantime, Conrad Grebel was apparently going through his own spiritual rebirth. His activities and letters reveal it clearly—Conrad had been born again. Historian Bender writes:

> Without a deep religious renewal such a transformation in the life of Conrad Grebel is wholly inexplicable. The external circumstances of his life continued to be most unfavorable. No stimulus to such a change came from his family or from his friends. He must have experienced a genuine transformation through faith in Christ. By the grace of God he was redeemed and made free from his own inner conflicts, from his old selfish and suffering life. He had found the salvation which he sought for his mother; "by the spirit of God he was born again, he had become a new creature, he had put on Christ." From henceforth his life was dedicated to a new master, to Christ the head of the church whom he now desired to serve as a faithful and devoted follower. He desires that Christians should pray for him that by the grace of God he may receive "the office of minister."[1]

Gone was Grebel's self-serving, sinful life. Gone was his idleness and pleasure-seeking. Gone were the strictly scholarly pursuits. Soon to vanish from his letters were his pagan oaths and allusions to pagan gods, goddesses, and mythology. Grebel had been remade into a new man. The record of his activities in the following months would reveal his new interests and drive.

---

1   Harold S. Bender, *Conrad Grebel 1498-1526: Founder of the Swiss Brethren*, 1950, Mennonite Historical Society, p. 79. References omitted.

The Grossmünster chapel towers over the Rathaus, the City Council House. The original Rathaus burned in the 1600s and was rebuilt. Note also that in Reformation times the double steeples had very pointed spires, similar to the smaller single spire at the rear.

Stress in the Confederacy and Canton

Following the violation of the Lenten fast and the Zürich Council's support of Zwingli, the other cantons in the Swiss Confederacy were less than pleased. In fact, at the meeting of the Confederate Diet (the representative governing body for the entire Swiss Confederacy) in Luzern that year, Zwingli's reform was the main topic of discussion. The pope had written a letter to the confederacy urging it to remain faithful to the Catholic Church. The Bishop of Constance, who had Zürich in his jurisdiction, was vigorously trying to hinder the Reformation within his bishopric.

While the appointed time for the Diet meeting approached, some of Zwingli's associates—including a couple of the sausage-eaters—met at Jacob Grebel's house to make a plan. Since Jacob was away on business at the time, Conrad was probably the host—and this would be one of his first known Reformation activities. Zwingli had recently returned from taking the medicinal baths at Baden, as had a couple of the men making the plans at the Grebel home. It was a custom of the Swiss that when those from the same hometown who had gone to Baden at the same time returned home, they should have a festive occasion at a local inn or home to celebrate their return and reunion. This was called a *Badenschenke*. Zwingli's supporters, gathered at Grebel's home, proposed a Badenschenke on a grand scale—with up to 500 people invited—as a public demonstration of support for Zwingli and his reform, sending a clear signal to the Confederate Diet. The plans were made and people were invited. Unfortunately for those who planned the party, the Council caught wind of the plan and shut down the proposed demonstration.

Grebel was soon to engage in more public demonstrations in defense of the Gospel as he understood it. His actions were to lead to another significant victory for Zwingli's cause.

Zwingli had been preaching lately against the Catholic idea that prayer should be made to the saints in heaven and that they could intercede to God for us. The monks of the city—who preached at the local monasteries and the convent—were quite opposed to Zwingli and preached against him from their pulpits. They were a stronghold of resistance against the Reformation, even as the Council (particularly the Large Council) was favoring the Reformation. In the summer of 1522, Conrad Grebel and three others—Claus Hottinger, Heinrich Aberli, and Bartlime Pur—dared to interrupt the sermons of the monks and even to take their pulpits. For this, the burgomaster—Mark Röist—summoned the four Zwinglians before the Council. Here they had to answer for their disturbance. During the trial, there was a loud banging heard in the Council chambers, and one of the councilors said that he thought the devil was in the room. Conrad replied, "The devil is not only sitting in the chambers but also among Milords ['my lords,' the councilors] for someone is sitting among Milords who said the gospel might as well be preached at a cow's hind end. And if Milords do not allow the gospel to go forth, they will be destroyed."[2] The council chamber was silent at the end of this stunning speech, and the councilors decided to "let them [the pulpit-takers] leave because they did not want to discuss the matter with them any further."[3] The four men were forbidden to take the pulpits, to speak against the monks, or to do any speaking or disputing on such topics.

The matter was not over yet. Five days later, a Franciscan friar by the name of Franz Lambert arrived in town.[4] The friar—who knew Latin well (but no German) and had been reading the Scriptures for 15 years—was allowed to preach four sermons at Zürich's Fraumünster cathedral. In the fourth

---

2   Zürich *Verbotbuch*, July 7, 1522; from Harder, Leland, editor, *Sources of Swiss Anabaptism*, 1985, Herald Press, p. 177. Used with permission. The councilor's words slightly modified, as they were too vulgar to print.
3   *Ibid.*
4   The Franciscans were an order of monks and friars founded by St. Francis of Assisi (1181/1182-1226). Friars were similar to monks, but instead of living in a cloister or monastery, they went around begging for money for the Roman Catholic Church.

sermon, he mentioned the intercession of Mary and the saints. Zwingli interrupted the sermon and called out, "Brother, you are in error there."[5] He did the same at the end of the sermon. Because of this, Lambert requested a debate with Zwingli. On Wednesday, July 17, 1522, at ten o'clock in the morning, Zwingli and Lambert faced off in the private barroom of the Grossmünster canons (the clerical staff of the chapel). They continued until two in the afternoon. At the end, the monk declared himself convinced, and declared that he would only pray to God and abandon the rosary.[6]

The matter was still not over. Later in the month, on the 21st, the subject was once again brought before the Zürich Council. The enmity between Zwingli and the monks came out at the hearing. Finally, the burgomaster gave the order that Zwingli and the monks must be cordial to each other and that any issues should be brought to the provost or to the Chapter.[7] Zwingli was not satisfied with this, and he called out: "I am bishop and priest in this town of Zürich, and to me is the care of souls entrusted. I have taken this oath, and not the monks. They should pay attention to me, and not I to them; and however boldly they preach what is untrue, I will counter it even if I have to stand in their own pulpit and contradict it. For we have no use for your begging friars, nor are you so regarded by God that we should have use for you."[8] A reform-minded abbot[9] from the Zürich countryside spoke in support of Zwingli. The Council admitted that in this, Zwingli was right, and the burgomaster ordered the monks to preach only from the Scriptures.

---

5   Bernhard Wyss, *Chronicle*; from Harder, Leland, editor, *Sources of Swiss Anabaptism*, 1985, Herald Press, p. 175. Used with permission.
6   A Catholic chain of beads representing a series of prayers—including more prayers to Mary than to God.
7   The authority over religious matters, such as appointing clergy for different towns and cathedrals.
8   Bernhard Wyss, *Chronicle*; from Harder, Leland, editor, *Sources of Swiss Anabaptism*, 1985, Herald Press, p. 176. Used with permission.
9   The abbot was the chief authority in a monastery.

Zwingli's struggles were not over. The Confederate Diet in Luzern had been convinced by the bishop of Constance to make a mandate against preaching Reformation doctrine. A petition signed by eleven reform-minded preachers—including Zwingli—was sent to the bishop, asking him not to make any proclamations injurious to the Gospel and to allow the priests to marry.[10] Following this, on August 22, 1522, Zwingli published a book—his most extensive to date—titled *Defense Called Archeteles [the beginning and the end], in Which Answer is Made to an Admonition That the Most Reverent Lord Bishop of Constance (Being Persuaded Thereto by the Behavior of Certain Wantonly Factious Persons) Sent to the Council of the Grossmünster at Zürich Called the Chapter*. It was one of his first significant pieces of Reformation writing, and defended his reformation against the bishop. At the end of the book, Zwingli included an aggressive poem by Conrad Grebel, "in gratitude for the Gospel recovered":

> Their fierce spleen let together vent the bishops,
> Such in name, but full truly wolves rapacious,
> For that now olden light of Truth again is
> Shining bright in the world with Gospel splendor;
> And this too by Divine direction, since the
> Lucifers triple-tongued and bold are conquered.
> Nay more (for I shall speak, a truthful prophet),
> Because now their dominion and oppression,
> Because now keys and canons, tome of Simon,
> Murders base of the conscientious people,
> For that this grim array of wares so holy,
> Their dear bulls,[11] thunderbolts, base superstition,
> All these things does the Gospel Word lead conquered
> And will lead in a glorious triumph always.

---

10   Roman Catholic priests took a vow of celibacy at their ordinations. Many kept concubines and in some places, communities would require their priests to keep one.

11   A bull was a specific type of papal document.

Churches, chapels, and cloisters

The Zürich city map to the right, made in 1504 when Conrad was a child, reveals the city's religiousity. At least 13 churches and chapels can be found inside the city walls, with more just outside.

One can get the idea that medieval Catholicism was one happy united church. Far from it! Historical documents reveal that the church was only united in an outward shell of ultimate obedience to the pope. In everyday life, the various monastic orders were in competition to gain the support (both in sentiment and in monetary donations) of the populace. Beyond the inter-monastic fighting, the local priests often felt that the monastic orders were drawing away support for the local congregations.

Conrad's home was probably the top dark circle on the map, although his father owned more than one house in the city. Felix Manz's mother most likely lived in the house in the bottom dark circle. Felix was the illegitimate son of one of the priests. Illicit relationships by the priests were common enough that some places required the priests to keep concubines (passed off as cooks and housekeepers) to keep them from seducing the women of the parish.

Such was the religious confusion of the day—a city full of churches, chapels, and cloisters, but without a clear testimony of righteous living and holiness. That said, there were some sincere and upright people within the State churches. It was this Babylonian mixture that the Anabaptists called into question, demanding that obstinate sinners be expelled from the church. While some State church ministers had the same desire for purity, they feared that expelling the sinners would leave the church almost memberless!

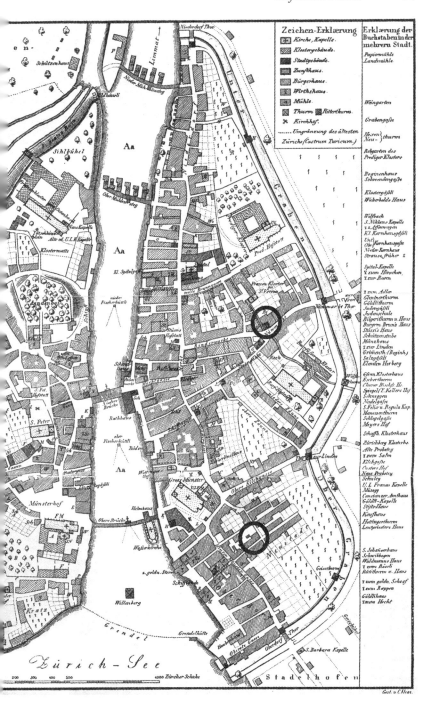

Such in name, but full truly wolves rapacious,
Their fierce spleen let together vent the bishops.[12]

Following the publication of this book and the controversy with the bishop, Zwingli resigned from his position of people's priest on November 9, 1522. Immediately, the Zürich Council re-hired him as the head of the Grossmünster Chapter. In practical terms, Zwingli's job did not change, but what had changed was to whom he was accountable and who held authority over him. He was now out from under the authority of the Roman Catholic bishop and under the authority of the state. He was accountable to the Zürich Council, and his reformation was to a large degree in their hands.

Grebel Transformed

On November 21, 1522, Conrad finally wrote again to Vadian, after a silence of nearly ten months. In this letter, the transformation of his interests, pursuits, and desires are clearly evident. His pagan allusions were soon to disappear as well. His earnest desire to participate in the restoration of the church and the defense of the Gospel against its enemies was given space in the letter:

> O my Vadian! If you knew me, how I burn with zeal to pursue this kind of wolves, how in truth the rest of my life would not be dear to me, unless I could worthily pronounce anathema on them from the gods above and below, lest you think it be from mortals only. And would that by the grace of God all would pray for me, that I accept this ministry in earnest and triumph in it. I add nothing more, since no wagons of words could

---

12   Conrad Grebel, poem at the end of Zwingli's *Archeteles*, 1522; translation by Edward Yoder, from Harold S. Bender, *Conrad Grebel 1498-1526: Founder of the Swiss Brethren*, 1950, Mennonite Historical Society, p. 281.

represent this mind of mine, which is to be discerned after the test has been made.[13]

Zwingli's reformation took another step forward when he preached a message to the nuns at the Oetenbach convent. This was a radical break with tradition, because only the Dominican monks were allowed to preach at the convent. Conrad's next letter to Vadian, written in December, reported the decision of the Council regarding those nuns who, in response to Zwingli's sermon, had asked permission to leave the convent: They had to remain there until Pentecost (at which time it was intended that the monastic orders in Zürich would be legally reformed), but until then, the Dominicans were not the only ones allowed to preach and hear confessions at the convent.

An excerpt from Grebel's final letter to Vadian in the year 1522 gives a glimpse into the state of his soul:

> Mother is quite ungodly toward me, toward my spouse she is even more rabid. I fear for her salvation, unless she puts on Christ and becomes a new creature born again by the divine Spirit. And the time begins to appear when many—would that it not include her also—eat the body of Christ unworthily and to condemnation if they have not in brotherly fashion forgiven the sins of others. O Christ, send to her, send to me, the ministry of Vadian, send one like Vadian, who by your truth may teach her to unlearn such ungodliness and who may teach me true endurance.[14]

---

13   Conrad Grebel to Vadian, November 21, 1522; from Harder, Leland, editor, *Sources of Swiss Anabaptism*, 1985, Herald Press, p. 190. Used with permission.
14   Conrad Grebel to Vadian, December 29, 1522; Harder, Leland, editor, *Sources of Swiss Anabaptism*, 1985, Herald Press, p. 195. Used with permission.

The First Disputation

In early 1523, Zwingli's Reformation won a major victory and received the official approval of the Council. On January 29, 1523, as Zwingli had been requesting, a debate was held between the advocates of the Reformation and the advocates of the traditional observances of the Roman Catholic Church. The debate was called by the Council, which would preside as judges over the debate and pronounce which side won. It invited the clergy—including the bishop of Constance and some other bishops—to attend. As it turned out, a representative of the bishop of Constance, John Faber, was the main spokesman for the Catholic Church against Zwingli, who was the main speaker for the Reformation. The disputation ended with the declaration of the council that "Master Huldrych Zwingli … has hitherto been much slandered and accused on account of his teachings, yet no one has arisen against him in response … or attempted to refute him by means of the Scriptures … no one has proved any sort of heresy in his teaching…." They made the following order:

> Therefore the aforesaid burgomaster, council, and Great Council of this city of Zurich, in order to quell disturbance and dissension, have upon due deliberation and consultation decided, resolved, and it is their earnest opinion that Master Huldrych Zwingli should continue and keep on as before to proclaim the holy gospel and the pure holy Scripture with the Holy Spirit according to his ability, as long and as often as he will until something better is made known to him.
>
> Moreover, all their people's priests, curates, and preachers in their city and regions and districts shall undertake and preach nothing but what can be proved by the holy gospel and the pure divine Scriptures. Furthermore, they shall henceforth in no wise slander, calling each other heretic or other insulting word.

Whoever then appears contrary and does not sufficiently comply with this, the same shall be restrained to such an extent that they must see and learn that they have done wrong.[15]

Zwingli's reformation was not only gaining success with the Council and other rulers, but also with the common people. A "Bible School" movement sprang up, as educated, literate men began teaching the Bible in private homes to whomever wished to hear. Andreas Castelberger, a.k.a. Andreas on the Crutches, opened one such Bible School in which—among other things—he "said much about warring, how the divine teaching is so strongly against it and how it is a sin."[16] At the time, Castelberger's teaching was similar to Zwingli's, and the Zürich Council allowed Castelberger to run his school. During the First Disputation, Zwingli stated that "matters have reached such a state that even the laymen and women [in the canton of Zürich] know more of the Scriptures than some priests and clergymen."[17] Although Castelberger and Zwingli taught the same or nearly the same doctrine at the time, they were soon to part ways—and Castelberger's Bible School has been called "the cradle of the Anabaptist movement in Zürich."

In the early summer of 1523, the nuns in the convent were given the opportunity to leave if they pleased. Zwingli's reformation had yet another victory.

---

15   First Zürich Disputation, January 29, 1523; from Harder, Leland, editor, *Sources of Swiss Anabaptism*, 1985, Herald Press, p. 198. Used with permission.

16   "Castelberger's Home Bible Study Fellowship," 1523; from Harder, Leland, editor, *Sources of Swiss Anabaptism*, 1985, Herald Press, p. 206. Used with permission.

17   First Zürich Disputation, January 29, 1523; from Harder, Leland, editor, *Sources of Swiss Anabaptism*, 1985, Herald Press, pp. 202-203. Used with permission.

The Tithe

In the meantime, controversy was growing on another significant Reformation topic—and it was possibly with this topic that Conrad Grebel was to have his first major disappointment in Ulrich Zwingli.

The tithe was a government-enforced church tax of 10% of a man's income. It was often used to pay clergy—sometimes absentee clergy. As early as 1520, Zwingli had taught that God had not commanded the tithe and that it should only be paid voluntarily. One historian notes, "as tithes were an important part of the ecclesiastical revenue, he was striking a serious blow at the further maintenance of the [Grossmünster] cathedral. No wonder that his brother clergy were alarmed. They knew all too well that voluntary payments of tithes or of any other moneys were sure to be small."[18] No doubt to the consternation of the other Grossmünster clergy, Zwingli's challenge against the enforced payment of the tithe caught on in the canton. In the summer of 1522, Simon Stumpf—the pastor at Höngg in Zürich—preached that men did not need to pay the tithe. One of his parishioners paid less than the full amount of the tithe, for which the Council imprisoned and fined him. In December 1522, the citizens of the town of Witikon called Wilhelm Reublin—a priest who had been expelled from Basel for his reforming activities—as their pastor. This was particularly bold, since the Grossmünster Chapter had the political authority for collecting tithes from Witikon and appointing clergy there. The Council decided that Witikon could keep its chosen pastor as long as the citizens both paid the church tithe and supported Reublin on their own. That is, the Chapter would not pay Reublin's salary out of the town's tithe—the townspeople would have to do that in addition to paying the tithe.

---

18   Samuel Macauley Jackson, *Huldreich Zwingli: The Reformer of German Switzerland*, G. P. Putnam's Sons, 1900, p. 156.

Tithes: tax for the church or for the state?

The early reform movement took various stands on the issue of the tithe, which was to support church proceedings. The tithe had been enforced for some centuries by the civil government. The serfs tended to despise the tithe, probably for two reasons.

1. They could barely scratch out a living as it was. Tithing was simply asking more than they could afford.

2. The tithe went to support people who tended to live luxuriously, and were often absent from the parish from which they collected money. Why should I sweat so the other could party?

But like it or not, the tax was law. Should a Christian break tax laws? The issue came down to whether a person felt the law was a religious law, or a civil law. Those who saw the tithe as a civil law felt that since the civil government is to be obeyed, then they should pay the tax even if the receivers of the money and goods misused it.

Those who saw the tithe as a church law felt that since the enforced tithe had no biblical support, they were not required to do what the Bible did not teach. Just like the mass was not biblical and could be rejected, tithing was not biblically mandated and could be rejected.

The question got really thorny, considering the mixture of church and state. Even if it was an church mandate, the state saw itself responsible to collect it for the church. Did that then make it civil law?

In some European countries, to this day a church tax is still collected. To get out of paying it, one has to officially sign documents stating that he wants to withdraw membership from the church. Otherwise, as long as one claims membership, a tax is collected by the government for the church. The church/state mixture is probably the reason for the disparity of views on paying the tithe, even among some Anabaptists.

In the meantime, Andreas Castelberger joined the chorus of criticism against the tithes and interest as forms of "usury":

He who does not have need, be he clergy or laity, but engages in usury with benefices [the pay which the state

Andreas Castelberger was an Anabaptist bookseller and ran a "Bible School" in Zürich. He was also known as Andres auf der Krücken *because he was crippled and used crutches.*

Laying up money = Usury?

So whoever lays up more money than he needs for his sustenance is a usurer? Such was the teaching of an early Anabaptist, Andreas Castelberger.

So how could he come to the conclusion that saving up money was usury? Simple. The early Anabaptists looked upon all possessions as being for the use of the entire brotherhood, regardless of who happened to have obtained them. Thus, if Brother A made $10,000 more than he needed for his (and his family's) sustenance in one year, that $10,000 did not really belong to him, but to whomever needed it. So, if Brother A kept the $10,000 to himself, he was essentially "borrowing" it from the needy, selfishly using it for unneeded things rather than helping others who had legitimate needs. By "borrowing" it from the needy, he became a usurer.

Most of the earliest Anabaptists held a view along these lines, with most of them practicing some form of community of goods. The Swiss Brethren developed more along the lines of "community of distribution," while the Hutterites also used "community of production" (meaning everyone worked together to earn the money). The difference was in how the goods were obtained and managed, but both models held that everything earned was ultimately to be used for the good of the brotherhood (and other needy people), not for the good of the individual.

Thus, if the individual kept more goods than he needed, he was borrowing from the poor, and became a usurer.

gave to clergy, funded by the tithes] and other things, or lays up more goods than he needs in order better and richer therewith to raise and feed his [illegitimate] children, and on the other hand a man with poor children steals because of his poverty to support himself and his children, then the one who steals because of poverty is as good and righteous in God's sight as those who have laid up so much usury and property beyond their need. . . . He, Andreas, also said he does not mean that the usurer should be taken to the gallows like the one who steals out of poverty; but in God's sight and as taught in evangelical doctrine, the poor thief is as good as the other man.[19]

Conrad Grebel also became opposed to the tithe system. While in Paris, he had realized that it was not right for him to live luxuriously on money from the king, which had been taken from poor laborers. He probably saw the tithe system as the same kind of abuse.[20]

The Zürich Council's decision regarding the village of Witikon was not satisfactory to Reublin's parishioners for long. Reublin taught against the luxurious and immoral lives of the Roman Catholic clergy, and in the summer of 1523, Witikon was joined by five other villages in petitioning the Zürich Council to be excused from paying the tithe. This conflict would soon result in another step in the Reformation drama.

On June 17, 1523, Grebel wrote to Vadian:

> There is nothing else that you ought to know from me, except that I grieve that Benedict [Burgauer], your bishop, has departed to purgatory,[21] as they call it, or rather as they wickedly contrive and dogmatically defend.[22] I always feared that political expediency might turn him in a direction other than what was either worthy of him or that I could consider good. May the author of the gospel accordingly overrule this departure for the better. . . . I would not lose hope that another laborer will succeed to the harvest of St. Gallen, and that this one at last will be sent from God.[23]

---

19   "Castelberger's Home Bible Study Fellowship," 1523; from Harder, Leland, editor, *Sources of Swiss Anabaptism*, 1985, Herald Press, p. 205. Used with permission.

20   Conrad Grebel to Vadian, January 14, 1520; Harder, Leland, editor, *Sources of Swiss Anabaptism*, 1985, Herald Press, p. 98.

21   See page 27.

22   That is, Burgauer had returned to preaching the Catholic doctrine of purgatory after having abandoned it.

23   Conrad Grebel to Vadian, June 17, 1523; from Harder, Leland, editor,

What Conrad had feared for Burgauer he would soon see done by his well-respected Zwingli.

On June 22, as planned, the Council gave its answer to the petitioners against the tithe: No. They were to continue to pay and furthermore were to keep quiet about the issue.

This was a serious disappointment to Zwingli and his followers. Up to this time, whenever matters reached a point where a reformation decision had to be made, the Council had supported Zwingli. Now, they were unwilling to act to abolish the tithe.

In his disappointment, Zwingli preached a sermon two days later called "On Divine and Human Justice." The sermon was an effort to deal with the disappointing reality of what the Council had decided. Zwingli argued that there are two levels of righteousness: There is God's ultimate standard of righteousness, revealed in the Sermon on the Mount, which men will not keep—indeed, which they probably cannot keep. This is divine righteousness or justice. However, there is a second level, the righteousness or justice of humans. This is a lower level of righteousness, commanded by God, which civil government enforces. Regarding these two levels of righteousness, Zwingli preached:

> The divine Word should rule over all people and shall be prescribed, proclaimed, faithfully published, and explained; for we are duty-bound to follow it. Only the grace of God through our Lord Jesus Christ can remedy our weakness. . . . But if on the other hand there are people who out of ungodliness and unbelief do not hear the Word, nor live up to it, God has given us lower commandments, not that by living in accord with them we may be righteous, but that the security of human society may be preserved and protected, and that watchmen may be appointed to pay serious attention to

Sources of Swiss Anabaptism, 1985, Herald Press, pp. 207-208. Used with permission.

it, so that even the last fragment of our poor human righteousness will not also be snatched away from us. These watchmen are the legitimate government, but it is no other than the one with the sword; i.e., the one we call the secular government, whose office consists in directing all things in accord with God's will [divine righteousness/justice], and where that is not possible, in accord with God's commands [human righteousness/ justice]. It should therefore abolish all things that are based neither on the divine Word or command nor on human righteousness and declare them illegal and unjust even for human righteousness.[24]

Applying this teaching to the subject of the tithe and interest, Zwingli said:

I say that every man is obligated to pay them [tithes] as long as the government generally orders it. The government may also punish the violator if he should refuse to pay it, for it is the consensus of the authorities; … Hence anyone who personally would refuse to pay the tenth contrary to this common consensus … would be resisting the government; and he who resists the government resists God, as shown before. But in a case where an entire government, that could defend such action, should permit that one need no longer give the tithe, such a government would also have to see that justice is done to those who hold the tithe.… But as long as that does not happen, everyone should pay the tithe as the government commands; and none should forcibly undertake anything for himself, or he would fall under the judgment pronounced on thieves and robbers.[25]

24   Ulrich Zwingli, *On Divine and Human Justice*, June 24, 1523; from Harder, Leland, editor, *Sources of Swiss Anabaptism*, 1985, Herald Press, p. 218. Used with permission.
25   Ulrich Zwingli, *On Divine and Human Justice*, June 24, 1523; from Harder, Leland, editor, *Sources of Swiss Anabaptism*, 1985, Herald Press, p. 213.

Council confusion

How did a city council get involved in deciding issues for the church in the first place? The problem was that the church was married to the state. The reformers were trying to deal with a mixture of the two kingdoms—the kingdom of God and the kingdoms of this world. If the church were separated from the world, as God has commanded, and allowed to govern its own activities in accord with the Word of God (tithe, Lord's Supper, baptism, calling of preachers, etc.), while obeying the government's decrees on other matters, the problems would not have been as tangled or vexing. This would have been infinitely better than trying to allow the world to tell the church when and how it could or could not obey the Word of God. Zwingli never accepted the idea of separating church and state.

Although the later Anabaptists agreed with the perspective in the above quoted lines, Zwingli seemed to have revealed the first hint of a weakness in his reformation activity—a tendency to give in too easily to the demands of the state instead of insisting that the church govern the matters of the church.

Conrad Grebel, too, was very disappointed. He wrote to Vadian on July 15:

What you have waited for so very much you now receive from Zwingli—the very Christian book by Zwingli; and you receive it as a gift. This for the present was what I had to write to you, unless you also want a report about the tithes. What shall I reply more frankly and truly and what more appropriately evangelical than this single comment which I now put forth, in a word: "The people of our world of Zurich are doing everything tyrannically and like the Turk in this matter of the tithe"? I said the people of the world, the tyrants of our homeland whom

Used with permission.

they call the senate fathers, but they should more aptly call them the decimating fathers.[26]

Despite his disappointment, life went on for Conrad Grebel and his famous brother-in-law. Vadian was growing into the role of reformer in St. Gall, even though he was a layman. Grebel and Vadian kept each other informed about Reformation happenings. In the summer of 1523, both had children born—Vadian had a daughter whom he named Dorothea, and Conrad a son whom he named Joshua. Joshua was actually Conrad's second son—his firstborn was named Theophil.

The Mass

Having been defeated on the issue of the tithe and usury, Zwingli and his friends moved the Reformation along to the next issue—the Mass.

The Mass is the name for the Roman Catholic observance of communion or Eucharist.[27] In Catholic theology, each observance of the Mass is a re-presentation of the sacrifice of Christ to the Father (that is, the sacrifice of Christ is presented to the Father again) and is a continuation of the sacrifice which Christ made on the cross. Furthermore, the elements (wafer and wine) used are viewed as literally and mystically becoming the body and blood of Christ.[28]

Zwingli set himself against this view of the Mass. He came to view the elements as symbolic of Christ's body, not as transformed into Christ's body. Based upon a reading of the

---

26   Conrad Grebel to Vadian, July 15, 1523; from Harder, Leland, editor, *Sources of Swiss Anabaptism*, 1985, Herald Press, p. 220. Used with permission.

27   The term "Eucharist" comes from the Greek word ευχαριστεω (*eucharisteo*—Strong's #2168), which means to be grateful or thankful. It is used in Matthew 26:27, where Jesus gave thanks before giving the cup to His disciples. In the Roman Catholic Church, the term came to refer to the bread of communion itself, with the Mass or communion service also called the "Eucharistic celebration."

28   See paragraphs 1364-1367 of the *Catechism of the Catholic Church*.

book of Hebrews,[29] he also repudiated the sacrificial view of
the Mass. He took up the subject in his preaching in Zürich,
advocating the reform of the Mass to remove the unscriptural
and offensive parts.

As early as January 1523, in the 67 Articles prepared for the
First Zürich Disputation, Zwingli wrote: "That Christ, having
sacrificed himself once, is to eternity a certain and valid sacrifice for the sins of all faithful, wherefrom it follows that the
mass is not a sacrifice, but is a remembrance of the sacrifice
and assurance of the salvation which Christ has given us."[30]
He elaborated in print again in July, and on August 29, 1523,
he published a book on the subject: *Essay on the Canon of
the Mass*. In this book, he made a proposal for the reform of
the ceremony of the Mass. It was a cautious book, in that it
allowed the retention of the priestly vestments, Latin chants,
and liturgical prayers.

After the *Essay* was published, some of Zwingli's disciples confronted him over the concessions he had made to the
traditional observance of the Mass. Although it is not known
for sure who these disciples were, there is evidence that they
were Conrad Grebel, Felix Manz, Simon Stumpf, and some
of the other thoroughgoing Zwinglians. They were concerned
that Zwingli had retained some of the unscriptural elements
of the Mass through a "forbearance, ill-advised" for the sake
of the "weak."[31]

Their biggest concern was with Zwingli's retention of the
vestments during the Eucharistic service. They argued that
the use of vestments was based on the robes used by the
Old Testament priests. This, they argued, would reinforce
the impression that the Mass was a sacrifice. Therefore, the

29   See Hebrews 9-11.
30   Article 18; from Samuel Macauley Jackson, editor, *Selected Works of
Huldreich Zwingli (1484-1531)*, 1901, University of Pennsylvania, p. 112.
31   Ulrich Zwingli, *Defense of the Booklet on the Mass Canon*, October 9,
1523; from Harder, Leland, editor, *Sources of Swiss Anabaptism*, 1985, Herald
Press, p. 227. Used with permission.

vestments must certainly be abolished. Secondly, they were concerned that leaving the Latin chants in the service would give place to spiritually dead ceremony and be an obstacle to the rebirth of a true Christianity. Thirdly, they argued that to leave liturgical prayers in the ceremony was a sin against God, because Christ did not command or exemplify a prefatory prayer before the observance of the Supper, and "whatever God himself has not taught by word or deed is sinful."[32]

Having encountered this constructive criticism, Zwingli soon wrote another book, published on October 9, 1523, titled *Defense of the Booklet on the Mass Canon*. In it, he recounted his unnamed friends' arguments on each point and gave his response. To the first point (vestments), he had never thought of what his friends had said about them; he had always viewed the vestments as symbolic of the abuse which Christ suffered. However, having seen his friends' point, he was quite willing to abolish the vestments (as soon as permissible, that is, for the sake of "the weak"). For the second point (chants), he was also willing to abolish them as well, preferring that they be replaced by preaching. Nevertheless, he was willing to be patient to await the abolition of the chants, as long as the texts sung came from Scripture.

> *Whatever God himself has not taught by word or deed is sinful.*
>
> ~Anabaptist principle

The third point was the only one on which he disagreed with his friends, and he devoted most of his *Defense* to the prayers which he retained in the liturgy. He wrote:

> Now I readily grant that whatever God has not taught by word or deed is a sin. For as he alone is good, so good cannot proceed from any but him. However, I ask what have I said in any of these four prayers which is contrary to the holy words? I should like one iota to

32   *Ibid.*, p. 229.

be shown which has not been taken from the celestial treasury, though in other words, so that everything may be both more simple and more obvious.[33]

The Iconoclasts

As the scholars were discussing the Mass, another Reformation issue was capturing the attention of the public—that of images in the church.

For centuries, the Roman Catholic Church had allowed the use of images and statues of saints or Biblical figures in their churches. Eventually, "veneration" of images was allowed. Allegedly, the image helped to focus the mind of the devotee on the actual, living saint in heaven as he asked the saint to intercede for him. The Swiss Reformers saw this as rank idolatry, and advocated the complete abolition of the images and prayers to the saints.

On September 1, 1523, Leo Jud—one of Zwingli's right-hand men and pastor at St. Peter's cathedral in Zürich—preached a sermon against the images, and said publicly that such should be taken out of the churches. Reublin in the Zürich countryside had already been preaching against images, and Ludwig Hätzer[34] published a pamphlet arguing against them. The tongue is powerful, and these teachings set off a wave of iconoclasm[35] in Zürich which was soon (at least from the Council's perspective) going out-of-bounds. On September 9, some of the officials at St. Peter's tore down some of the cathedral's paintings and statues. Four days later, at the Fraumünster,

---

33   *Ibid.*, p. 230.
34   Ludwig Hätzer was an interesting Reformation personality. He was a scholar and did some writing and Bible translating. He was involved with state church reform, but eventually was marginally involved with the Anabaptist movement, although it is doubtful that he ever received baptism. He was finally executed for adultery—a crime he admitted having committed, although he expressed repentance.
35   Icon- or image-breaking—the destruction of religious images. Today, this term is used to refer to the refutation of dearly held religious or other beliefs.

*St. Peter's cathedral in Zürich, seen from the towers of
the Grossmünster across the Limmat River.
The clock on the tower is the largest clock in Europe,
meauring over 28 feet in diameter.*

Lorenz Hochrütiner and a carpenter, having read Hätzer's book against images, destroyed the oil lamps hanging near the altar. For this offense, they had to sit in the prison tower for three days. Following his release, on September 23, Hochrütiner was involved in what was (to the Council at least) the most serious act of iconoclasm yet.

A miller found some of the Zwinglian radicals eyeing a large wooden crucifix[36] at the south end of town. Claus Hottinger asked the miller, "When are you going to get rid of your idol?" The miller said, "That is a matter that should be left to Milords."

Hottinger rejoined, "A good Christian would obey what Scripture commands and do away with it." With that, he, Hans Ockenfuss, and Lorenz Hochrütiner—all three of whom had been involved in the breaking of the Lenten fast earlier—broke the crucifix off at the ground and dug out the base. They planned to sell the wood and donate the proceeds to the poor.

The Council was not amused with their iconoclasm, nor pleased with their philanthropy. The trio was arrested. Later, at the trial, Hottinger said that there were three Council members who had encouraged him to do this act. Ockenfuss said that "one hears daily that such crucifixes and all other images of God our Redeemer are forbidden."[37] Hochrütiner said that "since other people had taken images of the saints and crucifixes from the churches and no one had stopped them, he thought that he would do no wrong."[38] The three were locked away to await their trial.

But the iconoclasm did not stop—it broke out at Höngg and elsewhere. The issue was becoming serious, and with the Council itself (apparently) divided on the issue, a solution had

---

36   A crucifix is not just a cross, but a cross with an image of the dead Christ hanging on it. (Compare with Hebrews 6:6b). Note that the graphic on the next page, made decades after the event, does not contain a figure of Christ hanging on it.

37   As cited in Harder, Leland, editor, *Sources of Swiss Anabaptism*, 1985, Herald Press, p. 233. Used with permission.

38   *Ibid.*

These iconoclasts put the wood from this cross to a better use—at least in their minds.

They chopped it up for firewood, planning to donate the money from the sale to the poor! The authorities had another mindset: their "generosity" cost the iconoclasts time in jail!

to be found. The Council appointed an 11-man committee to study what the Bible said about the worship of images and make a recommendation to the Council of what ought to be done. The committee was composed of four members of the Small Council (including Jacob Grebel), four men from the Large Council, and the three pastors—Zwingli, Jud, and Engelhart. On October 12, the committee made its recommendation—a public disputation was in order to settle the issue of images as well as the Mass. On the same day, Jacob Grebel wrote to his son-in-law, Vadian:

> I am letting you know that Milords, Councillors, and Representatives took counsel together just now. . . [to invite] again their lay priests and scholars in the city and their province, also abbots, plus Milord [bishop] of Constance, one burgomaster and councilor from the city of Constance, Milord [bishop] of Chur, Milord [bishop] of Basel, the University of Basel, and also all

parts of the league. They have been cordially invited for the sake of God and the Christian faith to appear on the Sunday before Simon and Jude [October 25] and then to assemble at the *Rathaus* [City Hall] on Monday to hold a disputation, especially concerning the mass and images and idols in the church. . . . It is therefore my request and desire that you, together with your cousin Jörg, brother-in-law Bartholomew, and whomever else you wish, will want to come. Bring them with you to my home and under no circumstances anywhere else. I hope you will not stay away and that you will be willing to take the time. If I judge correctly, you will not regret it.[39]

39   Jacob Grebel to Vadian, October 12, 1523; from Harder, Leland, editor, *Sources of Swiss Anabaptism*, 1985, Herald Press, pp. 233-234. Used with permission.

No, for Christian and brotherly love must be shown openly, each to the other, and it cannot be secret.

~Felix Manz's reply to Zwingli's question whether one could be a Christian in secret, by himself.

3

Disputation and Disillusionment

hile many of those invited to the Second Disputation did not come, Zürich held the debate as
planned. Ludwig Hätzer recorded the minutes
for the disputation; Vadian himself was one of the men presiding over the debate.

On Monday morning, October 26, the *Rathaus* was filled
with over 800 people gathering to hear the disputation. Burgomaster Röist opened the meeting and appointed three men—
including Vadian—to preside over the debate. The city clerk
read the invitation to the debate, and then Zwingli made some
opening comments. He said that the purpose of the debate was
to discern what the Scripture said about the issues at hand, not
to give practical instructions on how these teachings were to
be put into practice in Zürich.

The first day of the debate concerned images in the church.
Ludwig Hätzer, Zwingli, Conrad Grebel, and Balthasar Hubmaier[1] spoke out against images, while several others spoke

---

1   Hubmaier was a scholar of unusual caliber and a pastor in the Austrian
town of Waldshut. At this point in his life, he was a Zwinglian-style reform-

in favor of them. Zwingli implied that the images should be abolished without further delay. At the end of the day, Sebastian Hofmeister—a reform-minded pastor and one of the presidents of the disputation—expressed gratitude to God that the day had been productive, and that it had been discovered that images should not be tolerated. He pled for clemency to be shown to Hottinger, Hochrütiner, and Ockenfuss—who were still sitting in prison—saying that they had only put into practice what Zwingli and Jud had been preaching. Burgomaster Röist promised consideration of this plea when the three were put on trial—which would immediately follow the debate.

The second day was focused on the proposition, "The mass is no sacrifice, and heretofore has been celebrated with many abuses of its original institution by Christ."[2] The day opened with a speech from Zwingli outlining his view of why the Mass was not a sacrifice. He and Leo Jud then debated with some Catholic defenders of the doctrine.

After some discussion on the Mass, Balthasar Hubmaier rose and began to speak about images in the church. This might seem odd, as that topic had been settled the day before. Nevertheless, Hubmaier not only spoke against images, but gave a suggestion of how they ought to be abolished from the church. He suggested that the authority to plan and execute the removal of images should be placed in the hands of the local congregation, rather than in the hands of the state. (His speech was greeted with "amens" from some of those listening.) Recall that according to the rules of the disputation itself, the final decision regarding the practical implementation of each topic discussed was left in the hands of the state. Hubmaier

---

er, although he later became an Anabaptist. While accepting and defending believers' baptism and other distinctive Anabaptist teachings (such as church discipline), Hubmaier did not embrace nonresistance or separation of church and state. He was finally burned at the stake by the (Roman Catholic) Austrian government.

2   As cited in Harder, Leland, editor, *Sources of Swiss Anabaptism*, 1985, Herald Press, p. 660. Used with permission.

was suggesting that the church have the ultimate authority to obey God's Word. This would come up for discussion again later in the day, and would be a major point of contention in later years.

This set off a discussion regarding the issue of the jurisdiction of the council over the issues of images and the Mass. Further discussion about the Mass itself ensued, until the day was nearly over. Burgomaster Röist rose and said, "In the name of God! Since this point has been thoroughly discussed, Milords will be glad to grant it."[3] No dissent followed, and Röist began to adjourn the session. It was then that Conrad Grebel rose to speak.

The exchange that was to follow is one of the most famous discussions in Anabaptist history—and although it is doubtful that this discussion began the division between Grebel and Zwingli, it is certainly a hint of the division to come.

According to the minutes of the disputation,

> Then arose Conrad Grebel and expressed the opinion that the priests should be given instructions while they were still together how henceforth to proceed with the mass; for it would be futile if they did not begin to change the mass. Much has been said about the mass, but there would be no one who would be willing to stop this great abomination to God. In addition, there were yet much greater abuses in the mass. These also should be discussed.[4]

Hearing this, Zwingli replied, "Milords will discern how the mass should henceforth be properly observed."[5] This affirmation of the principle of the authority of the Council over church reform—which had been reiterated several times throughout the

---

3   *Ibid.*, p. 661.
4   Second Zürich Disputation, October 26-28, 1523; from Harder, Leland, editor, *Sources of Swiss Anabaptism*, 1985, Herald Press, p. 242. Used with permission.
5   *Ibid.*

day—was too much for the aggressive reformation preacher, Simon Stumpf. He spoke up and said:

> Master Huldrych![6] You have no authority to place the decision in Milords' hands, for the decision is already made: the Spirit of God decides. If therefore Milords were to discern and decide anything that is contrary to God's decision, I will ask Christ for his Spirit and will teach and act against it.[7]

> *Master Huldrych! You have no authority to place the decision in Milords' hands, for the decision is already made: the Spirit of God decides!*
>
> ~Simon Stumpf's reproof to Zwingli for giving the civil government authority in spiritual matters.

Zwingli replied:

> That is right. I shall also preach and act against it if they decide otherwise. I do not give the decision into their hands. They shall also certainly not decide about God's Word—not only they but the whole world should not. This convocation is not being held so that they might decide about that, but to ascertain and learn from the Scripture whether or not the mass is a sacrifice. Then they will counsel together as to the most appropriate way for this to be done without an uproar, etc.[8]

The day was done—the night was falling, and the burgomaster dismissed the meeting. All by itself, this little exchange might not appear to have much significance—but in the days ahead, in hindsight, it is clear that the division between Conrad Grebel and Ulrich Zwingli—between Protestantism and Anabaptism—could be seen, in seed, in this discussion.

---

6   Alternate spelling of Ulrich.
7   Second Zürich Disputation, October 26-28, 1523; from Harder, Leland, editor, *Sources of Swiss Anabaptism*, 1985, Herald Press, p. 242. Used with permission.
8   *Ibid.*, p. 242.

The Second Zürich Disputation in October, 1523

The next morning, the disputants listened to Ulrich Zwingli preach a message titled "The Shepherd," pleading with them to join the Reformation. At noon, they assembled again in the *Rathaus* for the final session of the disputation. According to plans, they were supposed to discuss the Catholic doctrine of purgatory on the third day, but the burgomaster opened the meeting with the words:

> Dear gracious lords, you presidents! You may now in God's name resume the discussion of the mass, For I well foresee that you will not say much about purgatory today.[9]

Vadian and the burgomaster then spoke some more, after which Vadian said:

> Let everyone who will, be he clerical or secular, speak against this article [of the Mass] today, but only on the basis of the Scriptures of God. Therefore, those of you who believe there are still many abuses of the mass

---

9   *Ibid.*, p. 243.

which must be discussed may now again bring them up and announce them.[10]

Following this encouragement from his brother-in-law, Conrad Grebel rose and began to speak:

> Dear brethren in Christ our Savior! Although it has been discerned and adequately demonstrated from the holy Scriptures that the mass is not a sacrifice, there are still many abuses which the devil has also added to this about which it is necessary to speak; for your mandate, Milords, concerns all the abuses of the mass. I therefore for God's sake urge those who can speak better—for I am not eloquent and have a poor memory—to be so kind as to open the subject here.[11]

Balthasar Hubmaier then spoke out against several abuses (viewing the Mass as a sacrifice, holding Mass for the dead, holding Mass for others, lack of true preaching, use of Latin in the Mass, and withholding the cup from the laity[12]). Zwingli then spoke out against chanting and vestments (giving acknowledgement to those who had helped him on these subjects). Grebel then mentioned that there were still other abuses, and he and Zwingli began a discussion on the finer points of the observance of the Lord's Supper—leavened or unleavened bread, normal bread versus round wafers, adding water to the wine versus using the wine undiluted, the priests putting the bread into the mouth of communicants versus them eating it for themselves, when it should be observed, the priests observing the Mass for the sake of money, and priests serving themselves the elements.

Zwingli and Jud both gave moving speeches at the end of the disputation, and the proceedings closed with several pleas for mercy for the iconoclasts who were still lying in prison.

---

10   *Ibid.*, pp. 243-244.
11   *Ibid.*, p. 244.
12   Roman Catholic priests served only the bread to the congregation, and drank the wine themselves.

The Results

The disputation was over—it was now up to the Council to decide how the proposed reforms should be carried out in the canton of Zürich. At the end of October, 1523, the Council issued a mandate with the following orders:

1. Pending further orders from the council, reform on the issues of the images and the Mass were not to be carried out. Images were to be left in the churches, unless someone had put an image which he owned in the church—in which case he could quietly remove it. The Mass would also be performed as before.
2. The Council ordered the truth of the gospel to be preached in the canton.
3. An introduction would be written which would be published with the proceedings of the recent disputation to further instruct the ignorant.
4. Several of the learned preachers were sent throughout the canton to preach the truth about images and the Mass throughout Zürich.

Although the Council had not yet ordered the reform of the Mass and images, they seemed to be definitely moving in that direction. Nevertheless, the forbidding of reform was, according to at least one contemporary observer, due to the Council's fear that if it ordered the removal of images and reformed the observance of the Mass, the canton of Zürich would quickly have a war on its hands—a war of all the Catholic Swiss cantons against them. The Council was opting for caution.

The disputation and following events were to have very concrete results for three men—the iconoclasts imprisoned in the tower. They were put on trial following the disputation. Lorenz Hochrütiner was banished from Zürich for life, Claus

Hottinger was banished for two years, and Hans Ockenfuss was released. Hochrütiner headed back to his native St. Gall, home of Vadian. Zwingli and Grebel both wrote letters of recommendation to Vadian for Hochrütiner, hoping that Vadian would be able to help Hochrütiner when he arrived. Following this, Zwingli wrote an "Introduction" to the findings of the disputation, and it was published along with the minutes and distributed to the clergy of the canton of Zürich. And then came the wait ...

Turning Point

Directly following the disputation, the Council had promised to give orders on the abolition of images "in the near future," and instructions regarding the Mass were to be "soon to come."[13] However, following the preaching tours and the publication of the disputation minutes, nothing happened. Nothing, that is, until mid-December, 1523, when an outbreak of demonstrations against the Mass and capital punishment occurred. Priests were taunted with names such as "the butcher of God" or "God-eater," the town gallows were vandalized, and liturgical books were stolen from the Grossmünster.

In response to this, the Council ordered its previous mandate to be read in the three main churches in Zürich, and threatened any transgressors with punishment. Several clergymen were appointed to "consult about the article on the observance of the mass and give advice on the position to be taken in the future on these matters at the hands of the councilors and representatives."[14]

Three days later, on December 13, the Council re-issued its previous mandate regarding the images and the Mass. The

13   Council Mandate, End of October 1523; from Harder, Leland, editor, *Sources of Swiss Anabaptism*, 1985, Herald Press, p. 251. Used with permission.
14   "The Turning Point in the Zwinglian Reformation," I, December 10, 1523; from Harder, Leland, editor, *Sources of Swiss Anabaptism*, 1985, Herald Press, p. 269. Used with permission..

War, or patience?

The City Council of Zürich was indeed between a rock and hard place. If they moved too fast with reform, it was pretty certain that some of the neighboring cantons would attack. Would you vote for church reform if you knew that it meant a war?

Hopefully, if the matter was essential to the Christian faith, we would be willing to follow Christ—cost what it may. However, if the issues at hand were not essential, practices that were not explicitly treated in the Bible, would it be worth a war to change?

Take, for instance, the issue of the minister wearing a robe. The Bible does not forbid wearing of robes, and Jesus almost certainly wore one. But suppose that the preacher putting off a robe would mean open warfare, with thousands of dead people. Could the preacher wear a robe to keep peace?

This was the predicament that the city council faced, only it was not one single issue, but multiple issues. If they moved too fast, it meant hundreds of deaths. If they moved too slowly, it meant part of the populace would be disgruntled with their decisions. Could a little patience save hundreds of lives?

The council ultimately chose to implement reforms at a slow pace, apparently to appease neighboring political allies. The issue could have been solved by a separation of church and state, of course. However, the position of the council is understandable, taking into consideration that in some cases compromise for the sake of peace is indeed godly ... in non-essential matters.

This same scenario has been played out thousands of times in church splits. Issues arise, be they doctrinal or practical. A decision must be made: should those who see "new" truths push ahead and cause a division in God's body, something the Bible warns against? Is the new truth "essential"? Is it worth a "war"of words and a split in the church, with hurt feelings on all sides?

In some cases, yes. In other cases, no. These are not easy questions, and in all cases patience should be exercised to the maximum. At some point, the needed reforms are more important than a division, but to define the tipping point is not easy. May we all walk circumspectly if we find ourselves in these situations!

rules were the same as before, but the mandate had two significant differences—first, it had a more aggressive threat of punishment for transgressors, and second, the promise for speedy reform of the traditional observances was conspicuous by its absence.

The Council called for a recommendation to be made by a special commission of fourteen men for how to go about reforming the Mass and the use of images in the church. The three people's priests of Zürich—Zwingli, Jud, and Engelhart—were members of this commission.

In the meantime, Simon Stumpf was apparently fulfilling his promise made at the Second Zürich Disputation: "If therefore Milords were to discern and decide anything that is contrary to God's decision, I will ask Christ for his Spirit and will teach and act against it."[15] He preached at his parish in Höngg against images, and the images were removed from the church—against the Council's orders. Zwingli and his fellow people's priests, too, seemed to catch the urgency of the situation, as the Council was shuffling its feet on the issue of the Mass, and threatening punishment against those who would take practical steps to reform it.

Simon Stumpf was to feel the wrath of the Council. On November 14, 1523, he was dismissed from his parish responsibilities at Höngg and forbidden to reside in the parish. He did visit again, however, and was arrested and brought to trial again. It was during his trial that Zwingli, with Jud and Engelhart, wrote a recommendation to the Council on how to reform the observance of communion.

It was also probably during the trial of Simon Stumpf that Zwingli was given a new suggestion for a path for the reformation to follow. More than once, Simon Stumpf and Conrad Grebel (separately) came to Zwingli with a suggestion of

---

15   Second Zürich Disputation, October 26-28, 1523; from Harder, Leland, editor, *Sources of Swiss Anabaptism*, 1985, Herald Press, p. 242. Used with permission.

forming a church separate from the entire society—in other words, a church of believers only, a voluntary church, not one which included everyone within a certain geographical area (like the Roman Catholic state church). Unfortunately, we do not have a contemporary account of this event, nor a sympathetic (let alone unbiased) one. The only historical record of these proposals we have comes from Zwingli, who by the time he gave the information was intent on discrediting the Anabaptists. Historians have debated exactly how much of Zwingli's description can be trusted. Nevertheless, here it is as Zwingli wrote it in his final book against the Anabaptists, the *Refutation of the Tricks of the Catabaptists*, written over three years after the event:

> For you must know, most pious reader, that their sect [the Anabaptists] arose thus. When their leaders, clearly fanatics, had already determined to drag into carnal liberty the liberty we have in the gospel, they addressed us who administer the word at Zurich first, kindly, indeed, but firmly, so that so far as could be seen from their appearance and action it was clear that they had in mind something inauspicious. They addressed us therefore after the following manner: It does not escape us that there will ever be those who will oppose the gospel, even among those who boast in the name of Christ. We therefore can never hope that all minds will so unite as Christians should find it possible to live. For in the Acts of the Apostles those who had believed seceded from the others, and then it happened that they who came to believe went over to those who were now a new church. So then must we do: they beg that we make a deliverance to this effect—they who wish to follow Christ should stand on our side. They promise also that our forces shall be far superior to the army of the unbelieving. Now the church was about to elect from their own devout its own senate. For it was clear that there were many

impious ones both in the senate and in this promiscuous church. To this we replied in the following manner: It is indeed true that there would ever be those who would live unrighteously, even though they confessed Christ, and would have all innocence and therefore piety in contempt. Yet when they asserted and contended that they were Christians, and were such by their deeds—as even the church could endure—they were on our side. For who is not against us is on our side.[16]

Assuming the reliability of Zwingli's testimony, his more radical followers—at least Stumpf and Grebel—were thinking along the lines of separating society into the church of the believers and the rest. The church of the believers, who would put into practice the teachings of the Word of God regarding communion, tithes, and usury, would—at least they thought—far outnumber those who wished to remain in disobedience to the Scriptures. In that way, a new Council could be elected which would support the Reformation wholeheartedly.

It was probably about the same time that Zwingli held a similar conversation with Felix Manz and Hans Hujuff. One night, Zwingli and Hujuff were discussing "a Christian people"[17] when Manz came to listen. Zwingli finally put forward the question "whether one could not be a Christian secretly and for himself."[18] To this, Felix Manz answered, "No, for Christian and brotherly love must be shown openly, each to the other, and it cannot be secret. [Manz] pointed out that Paul indicated when he wrote about it and said that fornication,

---

16   Ulrich Zwingli, *Refutation of the Tricks of the Catabaptists*, 1527; from Samuel Macauley Jackson, editor, *Selected Works of Huldreich Zwingli (1484-1531)*, 1901, University of Pennsylvania, pp. 132-133. A later trial record names Stumpf and Grebel as those who had brought the proposal to him and Jud.

17   Manz's term, in later retelling the story. Trial Record of Grebel, Mantz, and Blaurock, between November 9 and 18, 1525; from Harder, Leland, editor, *Sources of Swiss Anabaptism*, 1985, Herald Press, p. 441. Used with permission.

18   *Ibid.*

lasciviousness, and adultery and other things should not be tolerated among Christians, and a Christian should report such things." In response, Zwingli challenged Manz to do just that, and Manz responded that he was not a bishop—like Zwingli.[19] These events indicate that at this time, the Anabaptists-to-be were thinking along the lines of a separated church—one that was not a territorial church, identical with the citizenship of a piece of geography. They had not yet embraced full separation from the world, as they thought that this separated church could take over political power in the Council and enforce Zwingli's reform. Nevertheless, their concern at this time was for a way that the church could obey the Word of God on issues such as the tithe, the Mass, and images, and enforce said obedience rather than continually giving in to "the weak," as well as a concern (revealed in Manz's conversation with Zwingli) that the church be pure and holy, with unrepentant sinners being excluded.

Zwingli rejected all such proposals, and later used them (particularly Stumpf's and Grebel's) against the Anabaptists. He still held out hope that the Council would allow him to turn his proposed reform into reality, as revealed by his proposal to the Council written with Jud and Engelhart.

Between December 13 and 19, Zwingli and his fellow people's priests submitted a writing to the Council titled "Advice and Opinions on the Mass, announced by the Doctor at the Fraumünster, Master Huldrych Zwingli, and Master Leo, People's Priest at St. Peter's." It may be that Zwingli and his coworkers were afraid that the Council would still delay the implementation of reform, and with determination, they wrote:

---

19   *Ibid.*, pp. 441-442. Zwingli's account of this conversation was quite different: "Felix Mantz came to him once in front of Hujuff's garden and argued with him about the church, saying that no one could or should remain in the church except those who knew that they were without sin. And when he [Zwingli] asked Mantz whether he considered himself one of them, he gave him no real answer." *Ibid.*, p. 437.

Fourth, it is the sum total of opinion from the Word of God that one should present to the Christian people the body and blood of Christ with both wine and bread as a memorial of Christ's suffering, proclaiming the Lord's death whenever we use this food and drink.…

Fifth, we intend to hold a public observance of this [reformed] form [of communion] on Christmas Day, entirely according to the institution and practice of Christ, for we can no longer withhold the correct practice from the world; and even if they do not permit us, we must offer both body and blood, bread and wine, to those who desire, or otherwise stand [condemned] as lying by the Word of God.…

Accordingly, [even] if your love and wisdom would refuse to accept this proposed way, we know of no other way that would be so much in agreement with God's Word.… It is therefore our earnest opinion for the sake of God's honor that your wisdom might faithfully and fearlessly hold to God's Word.… Let God have control among his people, and whatever he commands, obey it like obedient sons, and you will not err nor be defeated. Amen.[20]

What might have happened if Zwingli and the others had stood by this determination in the days to come?

But alas, the decision was not in Zwingli's hands. Not even the fourteen-man commission went along completely with the three people's priests. They wrote a separate recommendation to the Zürich Council—a much less radical recommendation with much accommodation for "the weak." They wrote:

The preceding opinion presented by the three people's priests is without doubt the most correct and most conformed to the Word of God. Therefore nothing shall be undertaken in this matter that does not aim toward

---

20   Ulrich Zwingli, "Advice and Opinions on the Mass," between December 13 and 19, 1523; from Harder, Leland, editor, *Sources of Swiss Anabaptism*, 1985, Herald Press, pp. 270-271. Used with permission.

the point at which, with time, we will come directly to the practice of the pure Word of God.

However, since the hearts and beliefs of people are divided at this time—for many are still immature as we were in common a short time ago—it will be necessary to make some concessions to the immature until they can come to the age and strength for solid food.[21]

In the end, the Council adopted neither suggestion, except to allow that those whose consciences were offended by the Mass need not participate. Beyond that, no changes would be made to the Mass until further meetings, discussions with other political and religious officials, etc. had taken place. They announced that they would give the matter further consideration by the next Pentecost.

The door was closed—the council had put off reform once again, with no seeming intent to speedily obey the Word of God. Zwingli was once again defeated. Grebel was crushed.

---

21   14-Man Commission, "The Alternative Opinion," between December 13 and 19, 1523; from Harder, Leland, editor, *Sources of Swiss Anabaptism*, 1985, Herald Press, pp. 271-272. Used with permission.

"Not by accident, the cause of the gospel is in a very bad way here ..."

~ Conrad Grebel

4

Development of a "Radical"

espite his sturdy determination in mid-December, 1523, to "hold a public observance of this [reformed] form [of communion] on Christmas Day. . . or otherwise stand [condemned] as lying by the Word of God,"[1] in the face of the Council's refusal to allow such action, Zwingli backed down and continued to observe the old form of the Roman Catholic Mass. The parting of ways between Zwingli—tied as he was to the orders of the Council—and the others, who were determined to obey the Scriptures with or without the Council's approval—was inevitable.

The decision of the Council on the Mass, and Zwingli's attitude of compromise, was deeply disappointing to the thorough-going Conrad Grebel. On December 18, 1523, in obvious bitter disappointment and disillusionment with Zwingli's reformation, Grebel penned the following letter to Vadian:

---

1   Ulrich Zwingli et al., "Advice and Opinions on the Mass," between December 13 and 19, 1523; from Harder, Leland, editor, *Sources of Swiss Anabaptism*, 1985, Herald Press, p. 270. Used with permission.

Greetings, Vadian.

Since you request and even demand as my duty that I write to you, or rather reply, I have written as many things allow, [things] which seem to obstruct for many reasons. Not by accident, the cause of the gospel is in a very bad way here (if you can still believe a mistrusted one rather than a liar[2]), and it began when you with senatorial foresight served as president when the consultation was held. On that occasion (God sees and it is in his ears), the Word was overthrown, set back, and bound by its most learned heralds.[3]

Now I shall report how in dealing with the matter of the mass both councilor bodies assigned this knot to be unknotted to eight councilors, Zwingli the introducer, the abbot of Cappel, the provost of Embrach, and I know not what other tonsured monsters. They have disregarded the divine will on not celebrating the mass, and have prescribed a middle ground with diabolical (I know) prudence. This matter will be referred to both councils tomorrow, and so there will be mass. The pastors will see to that, etc. Farewell. Judge, but not as heretofore.

Axiom

Whoever thinks, believes, or declares that Zwingli acts according to the duty of a shepherd thinks, believes, and declares wickedly. When you ask for a defense of this axiom, I shall reply and send it.

On Friday before the festival of Thomas, 1523.

To the lord Joachim Vadian, most famous president of the Zurich Consultation, dearest kinsman.[4]

---

2   Grebel calls Zwingli a liar.

3   Grebel is saying that at the Second Zürich Disputation, at which Vadian was one of the presidents, the reformers themselves (such as Zwingli) hindered their own cause and the cause of the gospel by binding obedience to the Word of God to the decisions of the City Council.

4   Conrad Grebel to Vadian, December 18, 1523; from Harder, Leland, editor, *Sources of Swiss Anabaptism*, 1985, Herald Press, pp. 275-276. Used with permission.

Grebel was deeply disappointed, and apparently others were as well. On December 23, 1523, Simon Stumpf was banished permanently from the canton of Zürich. He had been outspoken and even aggressive in the implementation of proposed reforms. Meanwhile, a circle began to form around Conrad Grebel—a circle of brave men who in the course of time would inaugurate the Anabaptist movement.

In the first part of 1524, the discussions regarding the abolition of images and the Mass continued. Talk, talk, talk, talk—more and more discussion, debate, and recommendations, but nothing actually happened. Finally, in June, following the death of Burgomaster Röist, the Council ordered the images to be removed from the churches of Zürich.

A letter from Grebel to Vadian written in September, 1524, gives a glimpse of what he had been doing that year:

> You ask what it is I am doing. I am writing a reply to Andreas Carlstadt.[5] And I am writing for the first time to Thomas Müntzer (whose second booklet on phony faith I recently obtained and read). And perhaps I shall challenge Luther also, impelled by confidence in the divine Word. Then I am reading the Greek Gospel of Matthew to some pupils, interpreting it by my own abilities, not prophesying. Last of all, I shall list and assemble passages—judge these words without laughter and without that preconceived opinion of yours about the passages—indeed on two general themes; and unless someone else does it first, I will thrust these upon the public.
>
> Look at the reason for all my audacity: I have waited, and they have not spoken. They stood still and have not responded. I shall both respond on my part and declare the knowledge of God. For I am full of things to say, and the Spirit in my inner being compels me. Behold my

---

5   Carlstadt was a radical Lutheran reformer, some of whose writings the developing Anabaptists appreciated.

belly is as new wine without a vent, which bursts new
wineskins. I shall speak and I shall take a little breath.
I shall open my lips and I shall respond. I shall not
accept the person of man, and I shall not equate God
with men. For I do not know how long I shall tarry or
if after a short while my Maker will raise me up, hear
ye shepherds![6]

Babies—to Baptize or Not to Baptize?

During this time, the topic of infant baptism came to the attention of the radical circle gathered around Conrad Grebel
in opposition to Zwingli. It was not a new topic—as early
as July 1523, there was opposition to infant baptism in St.
Gall.[7] Zwingli himself had questioned infant baptism, as did
several other reformers, and Vadian seemed to consider infant baptism as an abuse which had to be done away with.

Resistance to infant baptism in Zürich began with a priest
by the name of Wilhelm Reublin in the town of Witikon. In
the spring of 1524, he began to resist and preach against the
baptism of infants. Under his influence, some parents from
Witikon and Zollikon refused to have their babies baptized.
As a result, Reublin was briefly imprisoned in Zürich, and
the Council ordered that any who refused to have their babies
baptized would be fined.

When and how Grebel and his closest associates, such as
Felix Manz and Andreas Castelberger, became interested in
the subject of infant baptism is not known. It is known that
Zwingli had brought up the topic in years past, questioning
the baptism of infants. Whether Grebel's interest in the topic

6   Conrad Grebel to Vadian, September 3, 1524; from Harder, Leland, editor,
Sources of Swiss Anabaptism, 1985, Herald Press, p. 283. Used with permission.
7   As testified to by the St. Gall pastor, Benedict Burgauer, in a letter to Grebel—Benedict Burgauer to Conrad Grebel, July 21, 1523; in Harder, Leland,
editor, *Sources of Swiss Anabaptism*, 1985, Herald Press, p. 223.

dates that far cannot be stated with certainty. But it is known that by early September, 1524, Grebel and his companions were thoroughly, firmly, and forever convinced that infant baptism was not supported by Scripture, and in fact was an invention of the pope and the devil. We know this by a letter which Grebel wrote for the radical group in early September as they sought for further fellowship.

The Search for Fellowship

In early September, 1524, the radical group in Zürich gathered around Grebel was aching for fellowship. Estranged from Zwingli and his closest followers, they believed that "Around here there are not even twenty who believe the Word of God."[8] How different from Grebel's earlier assurance that most of the Zürichers would be willing to obey God's Word!

In this state, they continued reading the current Reformation literature—particularly that literature written by men displeased with Martin Luther, disillusioned at the slow or nonexistent pace of actually making changes in the abuses which were being committed in the church. They felt a certain kinship with those who were estranged from Luther, as they were from Zwingli. They read the writings of Andreas Carlstadt, Luther's radical one-time companion, and a couple of booklets by Thomas Müntzer, also a one-time companion, now estranged from Luther.

Desperately hungry for fellowship, the little group wrote letters to Carlstadt and Müntzer. Grebel also wrote an eight-page letter to the Bible study group in St. Gall, which was debating the issue of infant baptism. Filled with zeal, they wrote a rebuking letter to Martin Luther, who never responded—he said he did not know what to say in response. Of these letters,

---

8   Conrad Grebel to Thomas Müntzer, "Postscript"; from Harder, Leland, editor, *Sources of Swiss Anabaptism*, 1985, Herald Press, p. 293. Used with permission.

Why the fuss?

Today, it seems almost a useless waste of time to argue about infant baptism. Even the churches that still practice it don't chop heads off over it.

The "fuss" in Conrad's day went a lot deeper than the salvation of the child. Baptism was tied to citizenship: no baptism, no citizenship. So to effectively renounce your infant baptism was tantamount to renouncing your citizenship. But not only were you renouncing your own citizenship, you were putting in question both the salvation and the citizenship of others. If infant baptism was invalid, then most of Europe was not baptized. And if they were not baptized, they were not saved, nor could they claim citizenship.

The civil governments had good reason to question the motives of those refusing infant baptism. In the late Middle Ages, peasant uprisings had occurred periodically, with grievances toward the nobility and church. Beginning in 1493, a loose peasant "movement" called the Bundschuh (Tied Shoe) movement had festered with similar grievances, sparking local uprisings. At the very time that Zürich was beginning to deal with the Anabaptist movement, outright rebellion, known as the German Peasants' War, was taking place in what is now Germany.

So when the Zürich Anabaptists began to speak of separation of church and state, renouncing their baptism, and similar talk, one can imagine that the civil authorities would begin to get nervous. Was the Peasants' War about to come to their territories?

The peasants circulated flyers called "The 12 Articles." Note how similar some of the demands (summarized below) were to what the Anabaptists were saying, especially the first one:

1. Every community should have the right to choose and remove a preacher if he behaves improperly. The preacher shall preach the gospel simply, straight, and clearly without any human amendment, for, it is written, that we can only come to God by true belief.

2. Tithes were to be used to support local pastors and the poor.

3. Serfdom was called a "shame" since Christ died for all and all are free in him.

4. Hunting rights should be given to all men, since God made all.

5. Community woods had been claimed by the nobility, and the serfs had to pay to use the woods that previously had been free.

A group of Bundschuh advocates confront a knight with a fancy headdress. Note the banner of the tied shoe, symbol of the peasant movement.

6. Forced work days (a type of tax) were being increased.

7. The amount of forced work days should not be increased beyond the initial agreement.

8. Lease agreements should be reviewed by honest men, since many of the leases had terms that were simply too hard to survive.

9. Fines and penalties should be held to old standards, not arbitrarily raised on the whim of the nobility.

10. Community lands had been appropriated by the rich, and should be returned to community use.

11. A common inheritance tax should be repealed, since widows and orphans had their goods taken away.

12. All the above articles should be examined by the Word of God.

As can be seen, the Anabaptists were saying some of the same things that these twelve articles were saying. However, the Anabaptist movement generally stayed away from fighting for their rights. It is interesting to note that all the peasant uprisings in those days were squashed by the lords, having accomplished little. In contrast, the Anabaptists patiently suffered without resistance—and some of their ideas (separation of church and state, freedom of religion) have now been incorporated into the constitutions of many nations. Their patient suffering won the day!

Almost Anabaptist....

Thomas Müntzer was a reformer who rejected infant baptism, but was probably never rebaptized himself. He was a leader in the German Peasants' War. Conrad and his friends wrote to him and reproved him for turning to the sword, but were encouraged by his stand on other issues.

only two survive—the two letters to Müntzer. These letters are among the most important documents in understanding the founding of early Swiss Anabaptism, and reveal the Grebel group's developing convictions around baptism, nonresistance, the suffering church, and worship.

These letters give the first extant defense or discussion of believer's baptism by the early Swiss Anabaptists. They reveal that although they had not to this date written about baptism, they had done much thinking and study about the issue, and had already formed the convictions regarding baptism which they would hold until death.

On behalf of the Bible study group, in September, 1524, Conrad Grebel opened their letter to Thomas Müntzer as follows:

> Peace, grace, and mercy from God our Father and Jesus Christ our Lord be with us all, Amen.

> Dear Brother Thomas.

Andreas Carlstadt was a reformer working with Martin Luther, but wanted to take reform further than Luther. In the end, Carlstadt was closer to Zwinglianism than Anabaptism, even though the Anabaptists published some of his writings.

For the sake of God, please do not let it surprise you that we address you without title and ask you as a brother henceforth to exchange ideas with us by correspondence, and that we, unsolicited and unknown to you, have dared to initiate such future dialogue. God's Son, Jesus Christ, who offers himself as the only Master and Head to all who are to be saved and commands us to be brethren to all brethren and believers through the one common Word, has moved and impelled us to establish friendship and brotherhood and to bring the following theses to your attention. Also the fact that you have written two booklets on phony faith has led us to write to you. Therefore, if you will accept it graciously for the sake of Christ our Savior, it may, if God wills, serve and work for the good. Amen.[9]

---

9   Conrad Grebel to Thomas Müntzer, September 5, 1524; from Harder, Leland, editor, *Sources of Swiss Anabaptism*, 1985, Herald Press, p. 285. Used

Repair, or Replace?

At some point, old tools are no longer worth fixing. If your hoe handle breaks, and a new handle costs $12.00, but a new hoe is only $15.00, will you then repair or replace? It will take at least half an hour to replace the handle, and besides, the blade is getting worn to a nubbin. It may simply be time to replace the hoe, rather than repair the handle.

This was the same question that faced the people of the 16th century. Basically everyone agreed that the Catholic Church was broken. Should she be fixed? Or, replaced?

Some opted to try to fix the Church from within. They stayed loyal to the Church and tried to bring about a genuine revival of real piety to the members. They were sincere in their efforts, and genuine in their belief that the thing could be turned around. Others felt the system could be fixed, but that it needed a thorough rebuild. The framework was okay, but most of the details needed to be rebuilt, more or less. The third group felt that the Church was broken beyond repair and needed to be totally replaced.

You may recognize the three groups, Catholics, Protestants, and the so-called "Radical Reformation," which included the Anabaptists.

Most people reading this book will probably agree that in the Anabaptists' situation, a total replacement was needed. But do you realize that almost every generation has to face the same question? Revivals die out. The Anabaptist revival has died out in many places and in various time periods. Those seeking a live church with a forward vision have had to make that difficult decision: repair, or replace?

Someone once said that the strongest opponents of revival are the leftovers from the previous one. In other words, those who have drifted to sleep, but think they are alive and well because they or their fathers had a revival *X amount of years* ago are often opposed to any fresh move of God. The problem is, they are convicted of their complacency, but are not humble enough to admit they have left their first love.

Each generation has to face the question. Each individual has to look at his church situation and decide: repair, or replace.

There is a time for both, and do not waste your time reading any books that claim to have a formula all figured out exactly when to fix and when to replace. Only God can guide us in our unique situations, and each situation is unique.

Walk close to HIM!

The rest of the letter summarizes some of what the radical group had in mind when they thought of the restoration of a New Testament church. While expressing appreciation for what they had read of Müntzer's writings, they felt quite free to disagree with him. For one thing, he had introduced German liturgy and chanting in the church—which the radical group, particularly Grebel, discouraged. In the discussion on chanting is found a statement of one of the guiding principles of the group in Bible interpretation and church reform—"Whatever we are not taught in definite statements and examples, we are to consider forbidden, as if it were written, 'Do not do this, do not chant.'"[10, 11]

The group also described their vision of a reformed communion service. They encouraged Müntzer to stand strong against the Protestant reformers' mantra of "forbearance" for the sake of the "weak":

> Pay no attention to the apostasy or to the unchristian forbearance, which the very learned foremost evangelical preachers established as an actual idol and planted throughout the world. It is far better that a few be correctly instructed through the Word of God and believe and live right in virtues and practices than that many believe deceitfully out of adulterated false doctrine.[12]

The group then described their disappointment upon learning that Müntzer had set up "tablets" with the Ten Commandments in the church. They pointed out that there was no word or commandment for such a thing in the New Testament, and that in the New Testament, the law of God was to be written on hearts, not on stone tablets. The Zürich group feared that setting up tablets would lead to idolatry and reliance upon something visible instead of the inner spiritual reality—the

with permission.
10   *Ibid.*, p. 287.
11   See the box on the next page.
12   *Ibid.*, p. 288.

To chant or not to chant?

Controversy has swirled around Conrad's strong condemnation of "singing" in the church meeting. In this position, he followed Zwingli, who held the same opinion. Some feel his arguments from Scripture are clearly flawed.

However, in fairness to Grebel and to the Anabaptists, it should be pointed out that the singing that Grebel specifically condemned was Latin chanting (the German word was translated as "chant" in *Sources of Swiss Anabaptism*). This chanting by trained choirs in a language unknown to the congregation was different from the a cappella congregational singing practiced by many of the Anabaptists' descendants today (and almost all early Anabaptists as well).

It is impossible to know, of course, what attitude Grebel would have had towards congregational singing as practiced by conservative Anabaptists today. As far as can be ascertained from the historical evidence, Conrad Grebel was the only Anabaptist to oppose singing in the church meeting. The Anabaptist movement as a whole developed into a singing movement, and their songs survive to the present and are still being sung by their descendants. Even Felix Manz and Georg Blaurock, two of Grebel's closest companions, authored songs which survive in the *Ausbund*. It is very possible that Conrad would have changed his views had he lived longer. But maybe not.

However that may be, Conrad's principle went far deeper than to chant or not to chant. He lived by the principle that *nothing is right unless the Bible specifically tells us to do it*. Most people, without realizing it, live by the principle that *nothing is wrong unless the Bible specifically condemns it*.

Have you ever considered which of these two principles rules your life? Most likely, the latter. Try living by the former principle for two weeks. Purge your life of anything and everything that does not have a definite positive command in Scripture. You will find that the necessary things of life are indeed given sanction in Scripture—eating, resting, and working. But you will also find that many activities simply cannot be supported by any Scriptural command. Is, for example, golfing commanded us in the Bible?

You may just find that living by Conrad's principle for two weeks will transform your thinking in such a beautiful and fruitful way that you will keep it indefinitely!

tablets would become a spiritual crutch. Nevertheless, they encouraged Müntzer:

> March forward with the Word and create a Christian church with the help of Christ and his rule such as we find instituted in Matthew 18 and practiced in the epistles. Press on in earnest with common prayer and fasting, in accord with faith and love without being commanded and compelled. Then God will help you and your lambs to all purity, and the chanting and the tablets will fall away. There is more than enough wisdom and counsel in the Scripture on how to teach, govern, direct, and make devout all classes and all men.[13]

They elaborated on their vision that the church's membership would be controlled by application of church discipline, as explained by Jesus in Matthew 18—not by the application of capital punishment. They described a church which endured suffering as a separate, minority entity in a hostile world. Only repentant, believing adults should be baptized, not babies. The letter was signed by Conrad Grebel, Andreas Castelberger, Felix Manz, Hans Ockenfuss, Bartlime Pur, and Heinrich Aberli. The group also wrote to Carlstadt and asked Müntzer to write to Luther.

While the Grebel group had hurriedly produced the first letter to Müntzer due to their courier's wish to depart quickly, events took a different turn when rain prevented his leaving. Conrad was able to produce a second letter to Müntzer, in which he mentioned that he had now written to Luther. Also, between the writing of the two letters, Hans Hujuff—one of the Grebel group—had been able to meet Thomas Müntzer. Through Hujuff's brother, the troubling information came back to the Grebel group that Müntzer had "preached against the

---

princes, that they should be combatted with the fist."[14] Grebel wrote to Müntzer:

> If that is true, or if you intend to defend war, the tablets, chanting, or other things for which you do not find a clear word (as you do not find for any of these aforementioned points), I admonish you by the salvation common to all of us that if you will desist from them and all opinions of your own now and henceforth, you will become completely pure, for you satisfy us on all other points better than anyone else in this German and other lands.[15]

With this fresh plea to Müntzer to change his mind regarding war, chanting, and the tablets, the Grebel group's courier departed with the letters.

Müntzer had indeed taught war against the princes, and was soon to become a leader of the Peasant's Rebellion of 1525 against the ruling princes. The peasants had felt oppressed by their rulers for many years, and in Luther's doctrine they felt they had found that God Himself willed them to be free from the oppression they were experiencing. If the rulers would not give them their freedom voluntarily, they felt it was their right to take it by force. They, too, were frustrated with the slow pace of reform in the church, and Müntzer believed that it was the "time of harvest," when the godly should root out and destroy the godless. After his troops experienced a strategic and major defeat, Müntzer was taken prisoner and tortured by the Roman Catholics, and he recanted. He was put to death by beheading.

Would things have gone differently if he had established contact with Conrad Grebel and his companions? Would Grebel and Manz have been able to convince Müntzer to establish a separated, nonresistant church, willing to suffer for the faith

---

14   Conrad Grebel to Thomas Müntzer, "Postscript"; from Harder, Leland, editor, *Sources of Swiss Anabaptism*, 1985, Herald Press, p. 293. Used with permission.
15   *Ibid.*, p. 293.

yet not fight back with carnal force? We will never know, for Müntzer probably never received the letters sent to him. They had sent the letters to his residence in Allstedt, Germany, but by the time they arrived there, he had already left the city.

While perhaps unfortunate for history, the move was fortunate for later historians; the turn of events preserved the letters for posterity. While the texts of the Grebel group's correspondence to Luther and Carlstadt have been lost, their letters to Müntzer were returned to Grebel. They eventually ended up in Vadian's archives, where they remain to this day.

Convictions Crystallized

By the time of the writing of the letters to Müntzer, the main convictions of the Grebel group which would guide them through the rest of their lives had crystallized. The following short months from September, 1524, to January, 1525, were—ironically—months when they themselves hesitated to take their already open break with Zwingli to the next step: the application of believer's baptism.[16]

It was not fear or idleness which caused them to hesitate. Rather, these months were spent in Bible study and in trying to get Zwingli to see the Scriptural truths they had discovered. Unfortunately for them, the months were also months of increasing alienation and hostility between them and their former teacher. In October, 1524, Grebel wrote to Vadian:

---

16   It is possible that at this point, the Grebel group had not even thought of initiating re-baptism of those who had been baptized as infants, but rather intended to discontinue infant baptism and inaugurate believer's baptism when those infants had grown sufficiently to confess the faith for themselves. If Zwingli is to be believed on this point, the Zürich radicals had never made any mention of rebaptism up to the time that the actual first baptisms occurred on January 21, 1525. If this is true, and the Grebel group had not previously had rebaptism in mind, it is possible that it was Georg Blaurock—who joined the group shortly before the first baptisms—who inspired the group to apply the doctrine of believer's baptism to themselves and accept rebaptism. He was, in fact, the first to ask for baptism.

Did I Get Any Mail?

If Conrad had written his letter to Thomas Müntzer in 2016 rather than 1524, when he was finished writing, he would have folded the letter, stuffed it in an envelope, sealed it, and stuck on a stamp. He then could have inserted it in his mailbox, put up the flag, and waited for the postman to pick it up and deliver it. Even Müntzer's recent move would not have prevented the letter from reaching him; with mail forwarding, he still would have received the letter. All for one low price of 47 cents!

We take our modern conveniences for granted, and even complain about them sometimes when they do not perform perfectly, do we not?

In the sixteenth century, there was no postal service. If you wanted to write a letter, you had to wait until one of your

friends (or, for upper-class people like the Grebels, one of your servants) was going to make a trip which would take him near your correspondent. You could then pay the courier (more than 47 cents!) to carry and deliver your letters and packages.

This system had serious flaws. Not all messengers were reliable; when Jacob Grebel attempted to send his son money, the letter reached Conrad, but the money did not. Couriers were sometimes slow, and letters could take months to reach their intended recipient. If no courier was available, you simply did not write any letters. And if one was available, but was leaving on a tight schedule, your letter-writing might be rushed. And because the system depended on couriers who were traveling long distances—and who wanted to be paid for their services—the poor had little, if any, chance to correspond with others.

Not only did the sender have to pay, but the recipient of the letter sometimes had to pay as well. Local governments sometimes collected tax on travelers traversing their territories, and the courier would bill these costs to the recipient of the letter.

Eventually, as the sixteenth century wore on, a crude postal service system began to develop—indeed, in some places (such as Great Britain), it was developing already in Conrad's lifetime. By the 1800s, postal services were noted for inefficiency, fraud, and abuse. In 1837, a proposal was made in Great Britain for a reform of the postal service. Part of the reform suggested that payment for letter mailing was to be on a radically new basis: The cost for mailing a letter, of any size and for any distance in the country, would be a flat rate of one penny, prepaid by the sender. Originally, it was proposed that pre-stamped letter paper could be used as proof of the payment of the postage, but this idea was revised to the idea of small, special pieces of paper, with adhesive on one side, which could be sold to letter-writers to affix on the outside of letters—stamps! On May 6, 1840, the world's first two postage stamps—the "Penny Black" and the "Twopence Blue," both featuring Queen Victoria's portrait—were issued.

Throughout the next decade, this idea was adopted in many countries. In March 1843, Zürich became the first government in continental Europe to issue postage stamps—the Zurich 4 and 6. The 4 rappen (unit of currency) stamp was for letters mailed within the city; the 6 rappen was for letters mailed outside the city, but within the canton. The United States federal government issued its first stamps in 1847.

Conrad felt that Martin Luther "walked backward" and was a "dawdler."

Like Zwingli, Luther did not take his reform program far enough for the ambitious Anabaptists. "March forward with the Word!" was Conrad's battle cry.

The most learned shepherds and they who seem to be pillars and leaders of the Word, as they are indeed, are they who drink the purest water and yet trample with their feet much water for the sheep to drink, in not a few places which still adhere to the faith. You do not believe, I know, with what disturbed feelings I learn of this, and what's more that I care nothing for the chief leader of the Word [Zwingli], who maligns me as the purveyor of envy [disguised] as an angel of light and hypocrisy from Satan. What is happening here is happening also at Wittenburg [seat of the Lutheran reformation], but the impartial reader will judge from the booklets of Carlstadt how Luther walks backward and how notorious a dawdler and vigorous a defender of his own stumbling.[17]

The Grebel group proclaimed the truth when and how they could. According to Zwingli:

---

17   Conrad Grebel to Vadian, October 14, 1524; from Harder, Leland, editor, *Sources of Swiss Anabaptism*, 1985, Herald Press, p. 296. Used with permission.

They argue in all the corners, streets, shops, wherever they can manage to do it. And if one opposes them in this and forbids it, they have fight-houses of their own where they slyly meet in secret, sit in judgment and condemn everybody.[18]

In return, the official Zürich preachers were harshly critical of their former students and supporters, as Grebel told Müntzer:

… our shepherds are also fierce and enraged against us, reviling us from the public pulpit as rascals and Satans turned into angels of light. In time we too will see persecution come upon us through them.[19]

In October, 1524, the radical group was busy with another project as well. Andreas Carlstadt seems to have been interested in the Grebel group (they had written to him twice). Although once an associate of Martin Luther, he had fallen out of Luther's favor for being too radical and quick in his implementation of church reform. In early October, Carlstadt sent his brother-in-law, Gerhard Westerberg, to Zürich, where he met with the Grebel group. He read several of Carlstadt's unpublished book manuscripts to the Grebel group, which became very interested in seeing these treatises published. They worked to raise the necessary funds, then Westerberg, Castelberger, and Manz traveled to Basel and found a printer, who produced over 5,000 copies of Carlstadt's books. Carlstadt himself came and visited the three in Basel before the printing began. One book, however, was not printed—Carlstadt's *Von dem Tauff* (*On Baptism*). Johannes Oecalampadius, Zwinglian reformer in Basel, recognized the radical nature of the tract

---

18   Ulrich Zwingli, *Those Who Give Cause for Rebellion*, between December 7 and 28, 1524; from Harder, Leland, editor, *Sources of Swiss Anabaptism*, 1985, Herald Press, p. 317. Used with permission.

19   Conrad Grebel to Thomas Müntzer, "Postscript"; from Harder, Leland, editor, *Sources of Swiss Anabaptism*, 1985, Herald Press, p. 293. Used with permission.

and intervened to stop its publication. Felix Manz tried in vain for three days to have it printed.

Despite this, the Zürich group left Basel with at least 5,300 copies of Carlstadt's books and distributed them far and wide. One of the booklets printed by the radicals in Basel was one by the title of *Whether One Should Proceed Slowly*. Carlstadt's argument against Luther's "forbearance" in this tract certainly encouraged the Grebel group in their impatience with Zwingli's "forbearance." Carlstadt wrote:

> Upon my report, dear brother, of some changes which occurred here, you wrote to me that for yourself you would like to move slowly hereafter, and through such writing secretly led me to understand that one should proceed slowly rather than quickly or suddenly in order to avoid offending the weak. You do nothing other than what the whole world now does which shouts: "Weak, weak, sick, sick, not too fast, slowly, slowly." Therefore I do not blame you … no one should look around at the other person or wait until the others follow when it concerns knowledge of the truth … when it concerns performance, we should do all God's commands according to our ability and should not wait until the foolish or weak follow. For God has always commanded that we all should learn his covenant and act accordingly.… See here! I ask you whether a son should not honor his parents until the weak follow along and also understand and want to honor their parents? You would always have to reply: "Certainly those who understand should not rob parents of their honor nor wait until all minors develop understanding and will." I ask whether one should not stop coveting other people's goods until the others follow? May one steal until the thieves stop stealing? Likewise I ask you in the case of all the commands whether it is fitting that we wait until the others have learned them

and want to follow them and do what God desires? Now just as I asked that about the commands which concern love of neighbor, so too I ask that about the works and deeds which concern God's honor directly.... I ask further whether I may blaspheme God as long as the others do not cease blaspheming? If you say yes, then the enemies of Christ and God may also rightly say that the murderers may murder, the thieves steal, adulterers commit adultery, and similar rascals engage in all kinds of vice until all rascals become pious.... What lord can tolerate it if he commands his servants to do something and then they all stand around and no one wants to be first or begin first? ... Because of the weak, they say, one should delay and not proceed at all. But is that not the same as if they said that we should allow the council to determine beforehand what we should do and to what degree we should serve God?[20]

Debates

The disputation, previously a useful tool for the advancement of Zwingli's reformation, was now turned inward—inside the reformation itself—as it was used by Zwingli against his former students and colleagues, the radical group gathered around Grebel.

The Grebel group and their rural associates such as Wilhelm Reublin were apparently having some success in stirring up public interest in the topic of infant baptism. Some parents now desired to withhold their children from baptism, and a stir was being created in Zürich. The Council gave a warning to these parents, but they stood firm and (as Grebel wrote to Vadian) "they asked for a judgment and pleaded and appealed

---

20   Andreas Carlstadt, *Whether One Should Proceed Slowly*, 1525; from Ronald J. Sider, editor, *Karlstadt's Battle with Luther*, 1978, Fortress Press, pp. 50, 52-54, 64.

to Scripture."[21] The councils then decided that a series of private disputations would be held each Tuesday between the opponents of infant baptism and the three pastors of Zürich. Two such disputations were held in the month of December, 1524. No official record of the disputations was made, and only partisan sources remain—Zwingli's accounts and Grebel's. Not surprisingly, both claimed the victory. Zwingli wrote:

> At the first meeting the battle was sharp but without abuse, as we especially took in good part their insults. Let God be the witness and those who were present, as well from their side as from ours. The second was sharper. Some of them, since they could do nothing with Scripture, carried on the affair with open abuse. When they saw themselves beaten after a considerable conflict, and when we had exhorted them in friendly ways, we broke up in such a way that many of them promised they would make no disturbance, though they did not promise to give up their opinions.[22]

On December 15, 1524, Grebel wrote to Vadian:

> Dear Lord Doctor and Brother-in-law.
>
> What you have asked of me I could not do.[23] Truth will not be bound to time. Therefore, understand it in the best sense. This is my wish, that it might be so. Others who have understood divine truth concerning baptism do not want to have their children baptized. They have been warned by Milords, but have stood firm. Then they asked for a judgment and pleaded and appealed to

---

21   Conrad Grebel to Vadian, December 15, 1524; from Harder, Leland, editor, *Sources of Swiss Anabaptism*, 1985, Herald Press, p. 301. Used with permission.

22   Ulrich Zwingli, *Refutation of the Tricks of the Catabaptists*, 1527; from Samuel Macauley Jackson, editor, *Selected Works of Huldreich Zwingli (1484-1531)*, 1901, University of Pennsylvania, p. 134.

23   Probably meaning that Vadian had asked him to change his position on baptism.

Scripture. Both councils then decided that all who say that infant baptism is unchristian and do not want to baptize their children shall present their reasons before the three pastors and the pastors theirs in return in the presence of four of the councilors. Zwingli and the lords appointed thereto have disobeyed all of this instruction. They summoned and abused the simplest one, yet nearest to God as God and the world know how. But with the help of God and his truth, he has put their wisdom to shame. Moreover, both councils have decided anew that they should meet together as previously ordered.[24]

Soon after the event, Felix Manz wrote:

I should have thought that all this would have been clear to you [the Council] simply from the truth itself, for your shepherds have often asserted that the Scriptures, to which we are not to add or subtract anything, must be allowed to speak for themselves. Although this was the intention, it was never carried out and we have never been given opportunity to speak, nor has the Scripture been heard, for our speech is cut off in the throat as soon as they suppose that we are about to speak the truth. They interrupt and demand proof from the Scripture although they ought rather to furnish such proof and stand by the truth—God knows that they act thus! . . . To speak is not pleasant for me, nor is it easy, for he [Zwingli] has already so often overwhelmed me with so much speaking that I was not able to answer or could not find room to answer because of his long speeches.[25]

---

24   Conrad Grebel to Vadian, December 15, 1524; from Harder, Leland, editor, *Sources of Swiss Anabaptism*, 1985, Herald Press, pp. 301-302. Used with permission.
25   Felix Manz, *Petition of Defense*, between December 13 and 28, 1524; from Harder, Leland, editor, *Sources of Swiss Anabaptism*, 1985, Herald Press, p. 312, 315. Used with permission.

While it will never be known who should justly be called the victors of the Tuesday Disputations,[26] Felix Manz's description of Zwingli's behavior does match some of Zwingli's own descriptions of the events. It is probable that, as happened later, the opponents of infant baptism were not given a fair opportunity to be heard. In any case, the Council decided to discontinue the Tuesday Disputations and a final, more public disputation was planned.[27]

> *I believe the Word of God simply and out of grace, not out of skill.*
>
> ~Conrad Grebel

Two days after the second Tuesday Disputation, Grebel wrote to Vadian:

Zwingli is writing on "force." … He, Zwingli, is writing also about rebels and rebellion; that may well hit us. Look out, it will bring something. May God prosper his truth and righteousness and put to shame all persons.… One thing I must say. To place in personal usury and interest and the splendor of this world a passing, fading consolation and security, or to be quiet about the usury of others, or not to warn about the coming sword: if this is to have believed and loved and forborne in a Christian way, then the truth of God is the most untrue untruth. The same applies concerning the present warring, forbearance, baptism, and the Lord's Supper. I believe the Word of

---

26   Nevertheless, a comparison of the arguments used at the time by both sides can be accomplished by comparing Zwingli's letter to the Strasbourg reformers of December 16, 1524, with Felix Manz's *Petition of Defense* written in December, 1524, to the Zürich Council.

27   While there is some evidence that there were plans for a whole series of Tuesday Disputations, which were then discontinued after only two, there is other evidence which seems to indicate that the Council only planned to have two. In either case, there were only two held in December 1524, followed by the more public disputation of January 1525—which also began on a Tuesday, possibly making it a third and final "Tuesday Disputation."

God simply and out of grace, not out of skill.[28] … For that reason may God give us his perfect mercy that we might obey, that you might submit to his Word without pretense and also obey accordingly. Otherwise, it is to be feared that the situation is not as good as we falsely console ourselves. The way is narrow. Too many vestments make it hard to get in.… They are going to write about rebels. They will be known by their fruits, by their expelling and consigning people to the sword. I do not think that persecution will fail to come. God be merciful. I hope to God that he will grant the medicine of patience.[29]

He signed the letter, "Conrad Grebel, your faithful brother-in-law. I would rather we be brothers-in-the-truth-of-Christ."[30]

The following day, Zwingli also wrote a letter to his reformation companions in Strasbourg[31] answering several questions they had asked. Among them was a question posed by reformers Martin Bucer and Wolfgang Capito about baptism. From this letter we get an idea of what arguments Zwingli was using at the time (and probably used in the Tuesday Disputations) to support infant baptism.

1. Zwingli argued that baptism could be used for those who had not yet come to faith, because John the Baptist baptized those who did not yet know Christ.

2. Circumcision, said to be a sign of faith for Abraham, was given to infants who did not yet have their own faith. Baptism is the New Testament

---

28   This single sentence from the translation in Harold S. Bender, *Conrad Grebel 1498-1526*, 1950, Mennonite Historical Society, p. 289.

29   Conrad Grebel to Vadian, December 15, 1524; from Harder, Leland, editor, *Sources of Swiss Anabaptism*, 1985, Herald Press, p. 302. Used with permission.

30   *Ibid.*, p. 303.

31   Then part of Germany, now in France.

replacement for circumcision, and thus should be given to infants.

3. Christ commanded that the little children should be allowed to come to Him. Therefore, we should do so by baptizing them.
4. The children of one believing spouse are called holy (I Corinthians 7:14). If children are already holy, they may be baptized.[32]

In December, 1524, Felix Manz—feeling that the Tuesday Disputations were unjust in not allowing him to make his case because of Zwingli's interruptions and taking too much of the time—wrote a petition to the Zürich Council, stating his case for believer's baptism and asking that they hold Zwingli to a written debate. Manz wrote:

> Wise, considerate, gracious, dear lords and brethren:
> It is well known to your Honors that many strange opinions have appeared. First, some hold that newborn infants are to be baptized as they come from the womb and that this can be proved from the Holy Scriptures, others that infant baptism is wrong and false, and has arisen from and been invented by that antichrist, the pope and his adherents, which is true as we know and believe from Holy Writ [writings–the Scriptures]. Among whom I too have been held and accused by some as a rioter and wretch, which is however an unjust and ungracious charge that can never be raised and proved on the basis of the truth, for neither have I engaged in rioting nor in any way taught or encouraged anything that has led or might lead to rioting (which all those with whom I have ever been associated can testify of me) . . . They [the Zwinglian pastors] know full well, much better than one could ever demonstrate, that Christ did not teach

---

32   These are his positive arguments for infant baptism. His replies to four arguments against infant baptism are contained in the letter as well.

infant baptism and that the apostles did not practice it, but that, in accord with the true meaning of baptism, only those should be baptized who reform, take on a new life, lay aside sins, are buried with Christ, and rise with him from baptism in newness of life, etc.[33]

In favor of believer's baptism, Manz argued:

1. John the Baptist baptized those who repented, forsook evil, and did good.
2. The Apostles understood the command to baptize in the Great Commission to mean that baptism should be given after people had been taught and received the Holy Spirit. He supported this with the examples of Cornelius and Saul of Tarsus. "To apply such things as have just been related to children is without any and against all Scriptures."[34]
3. No one was baptized in the New Testament "without external evidence and certain testimony or desire."[35]

Manz pointed out that he was sure that Zwingli "has exactly this same understanding of baptism and that he understands it much better than we. [I] do not know, however, for what reason he does not declare himself."[36] This point was made again and again by the earliest Anabaptists, and it has a basis in truth—Zwingli had, at one time, questioned infant baptism, as had many of the reformers.[37] Up to this time,

---

33　Felix Manz, *Petition of Defense*, between December 13 and 28, 1524; from Harder, Leland, editor, *Sources of Swiss Anabaptism*, 1985, Herald Press, pp. 311-312. Used with permission.

34　*Ibid.*, p. 313.

35　*Ibid.*, p. 314.

36　*Ibid.*, p. 314.

37　In his *Taufbüchlein* of 1525, Zwingli wrote: "For some time I myself was deceived by the error and I thought it better not to baptize children until they came to years of discretion. But I was not so dogmatically of this opinion as to take the course of many today, who although they are far too young and inexperienced in the matter argue and rashly assert that infant baptism derives from

it had never been brought forward as an important issue, as they were struggling with other topics—the Mass, the tithe, images, etc. By the time the Anabaptists-to-be became interested in the topic, Zwingli had already broken with them on other topics, specifically, how much the Council should be allowed to control the pace of reform for the church. By this time, it seems quite clear that Zwingli was genuinely in favor of infant baptism and opposed to believer's baptism, and that he was sincere in this belief and not hypocritical.

> *God wills that we keep his commandments and ceremonies, as he has commanded us.*
>
> ~Felix Manz

In response to the idea that "it makes no difference as to how baptism is practiced," Manz replied: "God wills that we keep his commandments and ceremonies, as he has commanded us."[38] The radical Zürich group was willing to fulfill God's will in this, even if it meant suffering. If no one else in Zürich would join them, they would have to do it alone—but do it they would.

Rebels!

That was the term Zwingli used for his former colleagues in December, 1524. His latest book, *Those Who Give Cause for Rebellion*, was released, charging four parties with bringing hatred upon the Gospel: 1) Those who listen to the Gospel only out of hate for Catholicism; 2) those who take the Gospel as a license to sin; 3) those who resist paying interest and

the papacy or the devil or something equally nonsensical." Ulrich Zwingli, *Taufbüchlein*, 1525; as cited by Abraham Friesen, *Reformers, Radicals, Revolutionaries*, 2012, Institute of Mennonite Studies, p. 100.

38   Felix Manz, *Petition of Defense*, between December 13 and 28, 1524; from Harder, Leland, editor, *Sources of Swiss Anabaptism*, 1985, Herald Press, p. 314. Used with permission.

tithes; and 4) Grebel's radical group, the opponents of infant baptism, who Zwingli charged as being "more inflated with knowledge of the gospel than ignited with love."[39]

The Breaking Point

The situation was not giving any promise of cooling off soon. The Grebel group was determined to obey the will of God, and Zwingli had publicly called them rebels. As the new year opened, the final point of departure swiftly approached—probably much sooner than Zwingli would have expected.

On January 14, 1525, Grebel wrote to Vadian:

> We are all well. Caspar Trismegander, the preacher at the hospital, defended infant baptism in the sermon to the preachers last Thursday. Jacob Hottinger interrupted him, but he behaved moderately and nothing has been done to him by Milords. However, a disputation has been set for next Tuesday in the presence of both councils, to which all who are for and against infant baptism are to gather. It will be announced tomorrow.
>
> My wife gave birth Friday, a week ago yesterday. The child is a daughter named Rachel. She has not yet been baptized and swamped in the Romish water bath....
>
> Zwingli and the Zwinglians have 96 theses in defense of the antichristian water bath. The clear light of day must be deceiving and blinding them. Until today Zwingli has been referring in public sermons to the bread and wine of the Lord as the very body and blood of Christ. No longer....
>
> On Friday, yesterday, he [Zwingli] preached a warlike sermon with all the trimmings, and the crowd applauded![40]

---

39   Ulrich Zwingli, *Those Who Give Cause for Rebellion*, December, 1524; from Harder, Leland, editor, *Sources of Swiss Anabaptism*, 1985, Herald Press, p. 316. Used with permission.

40   Conrad Grebel to Vadian, January 14, 1525; from Harder, Leland, editor,

Grebel was determined that his baby girl would not receive infant baptism. Zwingli was determined to hold the Reformation together and stop the "rebellion." The day after Grebel wrote to Vadian, the Council announced a disputation for January 17:

> Whereas some have expressed erroneous opinions that young children should not be baptized until they come to their days [of accountability], our g[racious] lords, the burgomaster, [Small] Council and Large Council of the city of Zurich announce that all who intend to hold to such views, be they clergy or laity, shall appear before them in the Town Hall next Tuesday at the regular time of meeting and shall state and prove from the pure holy Scriptures the reasons for their opinions, after which our lords will take whatever further action is appropriate.[41]

Like the previous "Tuesday Disputations," it was hardly to be expected that this disputation would be fair or evenhanded—particularly when the Council had already decided that the Anabaptists-to-be were holding to "erroneous opinions."

Strong George

About this time, a colorful character was to show up in Conrad Grebel's life—a new person in the drama that was to become the birth of Anabaptism. Jörg Cajacob, a former Catholic priest, now married, was one of the most energetic and impulsive men to be part of the early Anabaptist movement. While history has remembered him as a "second Paul," his character would suggest that "second Peter" would probably be a more fitting title.

Sources of Swiss Anabaptism, 1985, Herald Press, pp. 331-332. Used with permission.
41   Public Notice, January 15, 1525; from Harder, Leland, editor, *Sources of Swiss Anabaptism*, 1985, Herald Press, p. 333. Used with permission.

The January 17, 1525, debate with the Anabaptists in Zürich.

Cajacob was nicknamed "der Starke Jörg," or "strong George." Zeal characterized his life. Disillusioned with the Catholic Church, he had left the priesthood and married. Intrigued by the reports he had heard of Zwingli's zeal, he traveled to Zürich to visit with Zwingli himself. Upon meeting Zwingli, he was disappointed, but soon heard stories about another group of radical Christians in Zürich who were more zealous yet than Zwingli. Immediately, Jörg contacted Conrad Grebel and Felix Manz, and was extremely pleased at having found brethren with whom he could wholeheartedly join and agree. His addition was to have a profound effect on the beginning of Swiss as well as Hutterian Anabaptism.

Public Disputation

Jörg Cajacob participated with Conrad Grebel, Felix Manz, and Wilhelm Reublin in the next act in the drama of the development of Anabaptism: The first public disputation in Zürich regarding baptism, on January 17, 1525. Unfortunately, no minutes were kept, and it is impossible to know exactly what was said. Heinrich Bullinger, a young Reformed man (and later successor to Ulrich Zwingli as pastor of the Grossmünster), wrote the following account of the debate later in life:

> So a conference or disputation was scheduled by the authorities for the 17th of January to be held at the *Rathaus* [Council House] before the learned ones. Attending there in particular were the above-mentioned Mantz and Grebel, also Reublin, arguing their case that infants could not believe or understand what baptism is. Baptism should be given to believers to whom the gospel had previously been preached, who have understood it, and who thereupon requested baptism for themselves, and killing the old Adam, desired to live a new life. Because infants knew nothing of all this, baptism did not apply to them. For this they drew on Scripture from the Gospels and the Acts of the Apostles and pointed out that the apostles had not baptized infants but only adult discerning people. Therefore, it should still be done in that manner. And as long as baptism is not done in that manner, infant baptism is not valid and one should have himself baptized again. Thereupon Zwingli replied methodically in all of the comprehensiveness of his arguments and answers that he later encompassed in the book....
>
> After the conclusion of the disputation, the Anabaptists were earnestly admonished by the authorities to forsake their opinion and to be peaceful, since they could not support their cause with God's Word. But this had no effect on them. Then they said that they must obey God more than men.[42]

The next day, the Council officially declared Zwingli and his party the winners of the disputation and issued a mandate regarding baptism:

42   Heinrich Bullinger, *Reformation History*; from Harder, Leland, editor, *Sources of Swiss Anabaptism*, 1985, Herald Press, p. 335. Used with permission.

Whereas an error has arisen in the matter on baptism, namely, that young children should not be baptized before and until they have come to their days [of accountability] and know what faith is, and some have consequently left their children unbaptized, our lords and burgomaster, the [Small] Council, and the Large Council called the Two Hundred of the city of Zurich, have permitted a disputation to be held on the matter on the basis of Holy Scripture, and have decided that notwithstanding this error, all children shall be baptized as soon as they are born. And all those who have hitherto left their children unbaptized shall have them baptized within the next eight days. And anyone who refuses to do this shall, with wife and child and possessions, leave our lords' city, jurisdiction, and domain, and never return, or await what happens to him. Everyone will know how to conduct himself accordingly.[43]

On the 21st of January, the Council passed another resolution against the men who had opposed Zwingli on the matter of infant baptism. Their meetings were forbidden; Conrad Grebel and Felix Manz were ordered to stop talking about the matter and accept infant baptism; no further disputations on the subject would be allowed; and Wilhelm Reublin, Johannes Brötli of Zollikon, Ludwig Hätzer, and Andreas Castelberger were all banished and ordered to leave the canton of Zürich within eight days.

Although the Anabaptists had officially lost the debate, Jörg Cajacob gained something there—his abiding nickname, "Blaurock," meaning "blue coat," after the garment he wore at the disputation. George Bluecoat would play a significant role in the extremely important event which officially began the Anabaptist movement.

---

43   Council Mandate, January 18, 1525; from Harder, Leland, editor, *Sources of Swiss Anabaptism*, 1985, Herald Press, p. 336. Used with permission.

5

Missionary

On the night of January 21, 1525—the same day in which the Council had passed a new mandate forbidding their meetings and banishing some of them from Zürich—Conrad Grebel and his loyal brethren met anyway. Sneaking through the streets of Zürich, they made their way to their usual meeting place, the home of Felix Manz's mother.[1] In stately tones, the *Hutterian Chronicle* preserves and retells the holy events which took place that night.

> One day when they were meeting, fear came over them and struck their hearts. They fell on their knees before the almighty God in heaven and called upon him who knows all hearts. They prayed that God grant it to them to do his divine will and that he might have mercy on them. Neither flesh and blood nor human wisdom compelled them. They were well aware of what they would have to suffer for this.
>
> After the prayer, Georg Blaurock stood up and asked Conrad Grebel in the name of God to baptize him with

---

1 This was probably the meeting place, although it is not certain.

true Christian baptism on his faith and recognition of the truth. With this request he knelt down, and Conrad baptized him, since at that time there was no appointed servant of the Word. Then the others turned to Georg in their turn, asking him to baptize them, which he did. And so, in great fear of God, together they surrendered themselves to the Lord. They confirmed one another for the service of the Gospel and began to teach the faith and to keep it. This was the beginning of separation from the world and its evil ways.[2]

The act had been done. The break was final and irrevocable. The radical circle gathered around Grebel had become "Anabaptists," or "rebaptizers." They had pledged their entire lives to God and were not interested in turning back. Although Conrad Grebel did not know it, he had only about eighteen months to live—and the story had just begun.

The Mission Field

Immediately, the brethren went on the mission field. In this case, the mission field was the village of Zollikon, south of Zürich. It was here that Johannes Brötli, the assistant pastor, had resisted infant baptism. The village was ripe to receive the message of the Anabaptist missionaries.

The week following the baptism service in Felix Manz's mother's house saw great revival in Zollikon.[3] Grebel and Manz preached morning and evening. In about a week's time, there were at least 35 baptisms. While Zwingli was still chanting the Mass in the Grossmünster, the Anabaptists of Zollikon held several communion services in apostolic simplicity.

---

2   *The Chronicle of the Hutterian Brethren, Volume I*, Plough Publishing House, 1987, p. 45.

3   The history of the Zollikon Anabaptist congregation is well-told in Fritz Blanke's classic, *Brothers in Christ*, Herald Press, 1961. The story is dramatized in Joseph Stoll's excellent book, *Fire in the Zürich Hills*, 1973, Pathway Publishing, available from Sermon on the Mount Publishing.

The house on the left is believed to be the house where Felix Manz lived with his mother, the scene of the first rebaptisms in Zürich. The spires of the Grossmünster can be seen rising in the background.

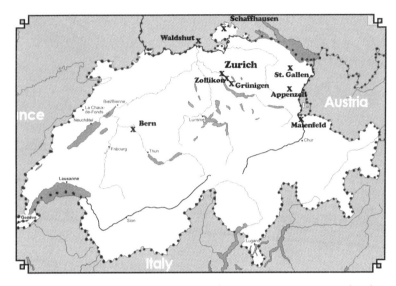

Within a couple of years, Anabaptist missionaries had visited a number of other Swiss towns, baptizing and establishing new congregations.

On Monday morning, January 30, tragedy struck the young congregation. Due in part to a disturbance caused by Blaurock in the Reformed church on Sunday, 25 Zollikon Anabaptists as well as Manz and Blaurock were arrested by Zürich officials and imprisoned in the city. Sadly, the Zollikoners recanted and were released, while Manz and Blaurock stayed steadfast and were kept in prison. Conrad Grebel, in the meantime, had gone to Schaffhausen, north-northeast of Zürich.

Schaffhausen

Probably before the end of January, 1525, Conrad Grebel departed for Schaffhausen, north of Zürich. Here he began evangelizing. Johannes Brötli and Wilhelm Reublin, on their way out of Zürich, met him there briefly. In March, Grebel baptized a man by the name of Wolfgang Ulimann, who would later himself become a missionary and martyr. Ulimann had been a Zwinglian before, but had questioned infant baptism due to the influence of Lorenz Hochrütiner (who had been banished from Zürich for iconoclasm). Being taught about believer's baptism by Grebel, Ulimann "was so thoroughly convinced by [Grebel] in favor of rebaptism that he would not have merely a pan of water poured over him but ... was pushed under and immersed in the Rhine by Grebel."[4]

Grebel's specific mission in Schaffhausen was to win the local pastors. He met with Dr. Sebastian Hofmeister, the chief pastor, and Dr. Sebastian Meyer. While Brötli and Reublin were in Schaffhausen with him, Grebel visited with the two pastors, and the three Anabaptists had dinner with them one evening. The next day, Brötli and Reublin went their separate ways—Brötli to Hallau, also in the canton Schaffhausen, where he established a congregation, and Reublin to Waldshut in southern Germany, where he was the guest of Dr. Balthasar Hubmaier.

During his brief stay, Grebel was able to influence Hofmeister to a great degree. Brötli received a distinct impression that "Dr. Sebastian was of one mind with us regarding baptism."[5] Balthasar Hubmaier later testified that Hofmeister had written him a letter stating:

> Therefore, we have not been ashamed of the truth, but publicly we have confessed before the Council at Schaffhausen that our brother Zwingli, if he would want that children must be baptized, errs from the goal and does not walk according to the truth of the gospel. Truly I could not be forced to baptize my child. Accordingly, you [Hubmaier and the Anabaptists] act in a Christian fashion when you again bring forth the true baptism of Christ which has long lain neglected. We would also

4   Johannes Kessler, *Sabbata*; from Harder, Leland, editor, *Sources of Swiss Anabaptism*, 1985, Herald Press, p. 360. Used with permission.
5   Johannes Brötli to the congregation at Zollikon, after February 5, 1525; from Harder, Leland, editor, *Sources of Swiss Anabaptism*, 1985, Herald Press, p. 351. Used with permission.

undertake such. May God give grace to your and our enterprise, that it come out well.[6]

Hofmeister also preached against infant baptism from the pulpit. A disputation on the subject of infant baptism was planned in Schaffhausen, but when Zürich found out about it, they ordered the disputation to be called off. For his preaching on baptism, Hofmeister was expelled from Schaffhausen in August.

Grebel's stay in Schaffhausen only lasted until sometime in March, 1525. While still in Schaffhausen, he gave a document containing a collection of Scriptures against infant baptism to a man he had been trying to convert. This found its way into Zwingli's hands, who threatened to refute it. At the same time, Grebel had nearly succeeded in winning a young Frenchman by the name of Anemund de Coct. However, de Coct decided to confer with Zwingli himself, and was completely turned against Grebel. Grebel later said that "he had known that if he [de Coct] went to Zwingli the latter would put his poison into him also."[7] de Coct soon became seriously ill and died in Hofmeister's home.

Second Disputation

While Grebel was evangelizing in Schaffhausen, Felix Manz, who had been imprisoned since February, and Georg Blaurock, who had been in prison for several days, were called upon to defend themselves and their doctrine in a public disputation—the second public disputation on baptism. Unfortunately, no minutes were kept, although a few bits of dialogue were reported by Zwingli in a later book. The dis-

6   Balthasar Hubmaier, *Old and New Teachers on Believers Baptism*, 1526; from Pipkin, H. Wayne, John H. Yoder, translation and editing, *Balthasar Hubmaier: Theologian of Anabaptism*. 1989, Herald Press, pp. 258-259. Used with permission.

7   Harold S. Bender, *Conrad Grebel 1498-1526: Founder of the Swiss Brethren*, 1950, Mennonite Historical Society, p. 142.

putation lasted three days, March 20-22, 1525. The Zwinglian preachers, of course, claimed the victory, and the council ordered the Anabaptists to forsake their beliefs. The Anabaptists, in turn, said that they would prove their doctrine by blood. A round of banishments and imprisonments followed.

Not long after the disputation—or perhaps during the disputation itself—Grebel returned to Zürich. The only clue we have to his presence is a letter from Zwingli to Vadian, in which he states:

> Grebel is among us, everywhere drawing to his faction whomever he can, and so reproaching and slandering our ministry that, even if we were at all the sort that he declares, still it was least of all fitting for him to be so ungrateful to one who deserves better.[8]

Zwingli may have known that St. Gall was Grebel's next destination, for he then wrote: "Strengthen yourself, lest you be seduced by his opinion; for he has this peculiarity, that he is silent about those very things which we present, yelping his own."[9] Zwingli went on to tell Vadian that he intended soon to write a book on baptism, and boasted that his intended interpretation had never been held by anyone else throughout all of church history:

> The next task … will be on baptism, which I will treat very differently from the way any ancient or modern writers have treated it, although it is not I who will treat it that way but the Word itself, which nevertheless must be interpreted differently than has been done so far.[10]

---

8   Ulrich Zwingli to Vadian, March 31, 1525; from Harder, Leland, editor, *Sources of Swiss Anabaptism*, 1985, Herald Press, p. 356. Used with permission.
9   *Ibid.*
10   *Ibid.*

St. Gall

Grebel's next mission field was St. Gall, the home of his beloved Vadian. We know from Grebel's letters that one of his greatest hopes was to win Vadian to his cause. However, his primary goal in St. Gall was probably to help the fledgling Anabaptist movement in the city. Led by Wolfgang Ulimann, there were a growing number of people influenced to abandon infant baptism. They were meeting by themselves in homes or outdoors. Grebel arrived on March 25, and on Palm Sunday, a great procession streamed to the Sitter River, where they were baptized by Grebel.

Grebel stayed in St. Gall for two weeks. Following the baptism, he preached to great crowds in the Weaver's Hall in the city. Grebel left the congregation in the care of Wolfgang Ulimann and another man by the name of Bolt Eberli. Some of the Zollikon Anabaptists soon arrived in St. Gall as well.

Back in Zürich

Grebel returned to his home in Zürich following his successful mission in St. Gall. On his way there, he stopped briefly at the town of Oberwinterthur. While there, the brother-in-law of Grebel's friend and fellow-Anabaptist Marx Bosshart, a man by the name of Arbogast Finsterbach, asked Grebel what he had to do in order to be baptized. Grebel replied: "One must first give up fornication, gambling, drinking, and usury."[11]

When Grebel arrived back in his home city—the city where Zwingli was—he laid low and quiet, avoiding arrest. Felix Manz was also staying in Grebel's home.

Grebel needed to pay off his debts, and he arranged to accomplish this during his stay in the city. He cataloged his library and sent the list to Andreas Castelberger, who was himself

_____

11   Harold S. Bender, *Conrad Grebel 1498-1526: Founder of the Swiss Brethren*, 1950, Mennonite Historical Society, p. 146.

When the whole world falls apart

Conrad's "holokosmos" ended up being a grief to him. When he wanted to go forth preaching, Barbara threatened to tell the authorities of Felix Manz's whereabouts. It is not known how much Barbara did support Conrad. Evidently she went along with not getting their children baptized. No records show that she ever received believer's baptism.

The new Anabaptist movement was in its infancy, finding its way through various issues. Had Conrad lived longer, his wife's apparent disloyalty probably would have disqualified him from receiving ordination. For all its strengths, the early Anabaptist movement had some weak spots in its founding as well, like all revival movements have had.

preparing to leave Zürich permanently due to his banishment. He asked Andreas, who was a bookseller, to find a buyer for his library. His letter to Andreas reveals that he was drawing comfort from the book of Revelation while he and his were experiencing persecution.

Another complicating factor in his stay in Zürich was his wife Barbara, whom he had once called his *Holokosmos* ("whole world"). Barbara never embraced the faith of her husband, and seems to have been highly displeased by his far-ranging missionary activity. Before writing his letter to Castelberger, Grebel had tried to leave the city, but Barbara thwarted his attempt, as described by Grebel to Castelberger:

> I had written to you that I was going away. I was going along with Felix Mantz, preparing to leave by night on Sunday. Then my wife (how Satan never rests) said she would betray Felix, who on the previous night had left my house again and gone to his own to await me there. I disregarded the great insolence of Eve and went out. She went out through another door to father's house, where she stirred up no small tragedy over my departure.

In the meanwhile I come to the gate nearest me, which was locked. I go up to the neighboring one, with fear of being recognized. I wanted to be cautious. I knocked to have it opened. Then Lady Meis calls to me from her house saying that no one was being let out through that gate (which was also true), as it was for me at the Neumarkt gate. On my return I pray the Lord to show me what would be the best thing to do. It occurred to me at once on the way back to my house that if I should later be banished or Felix betrayed by my wife, the possibility for the brothers from Zollikon to come secretly might be cut off through the placing of guards. By then I barely hobbled along because the sores on my feet hindered me. For the third time the closing of a gate held me back. So I have returned and await something else from the Lord.[12]

The Movement Expands in St. Gall

In the meantime, the movement was gaining great strength in St. Gall. Bolt Eberli had preached to great crowds and received baptism. The city council, which was uneasy about the movement but at that time was not inclined to suppress Anabaptism altogether, finally requested that Eberli leave on April 21. (St. Gall was still officially Catholic, although there was a Zwinglian party in the canton in addition to the Anabaptists.) Having reached his home in the Catholic canton of Schwyz, he was promptly arrested, sentenced to death, and burned at the stake with an ex-priest whose identity remains unknown. On May 29, 1525, he became the first Anabaptist martyr.

With Wolfgang Ulimann to continue leading the Anabaptists in St. Gall, however, Eberli's departure and eventual

12   Conrad Grebel to Andreas Castelberger, April 25, 1525; from Harder, Leland, editor, *Sources of Swiss Anabaptism*, 1985, Herald Press, p. 357. Used with permission.

martyrdom did not slow down the movement. The Anabaptists found a small hut near one of the city gates where they held meetings almost every evening. The Protestant party in the city was continually losing members to the Anabaptists. After a critical description of their meetings, the St. Gall chronicler and Protestant supporter Johannes Kessler described the lives of the early Anabaptists in St. Gall:

> At the same time their conduct and attitude seemed quite pious, holy, and blameless. They avoided costly clothing, despised costly food and drink, dressed in coarse material, covered their heads with broad felt hats, their walk and life very humble. They carried no gun or sword or dagger, except a broken-off bread knife. They said the former were wolves' clothing which the sheep should not wear. They did not swear, not even the obligatory civil oath to the government. And if one transgressed herein, he was banned by them, for there was daily excommunication among them.[13]

Due to the increasing loss of Protestants to the Anabaptists, the Council of St. Gall ordered that the Anabaptists could preach, as long as they did it in the established church buildings and not in irregular places. (Ulimann had a conviction against this due to the images and idols in the church buildings.) In response, Ulimann preached a hot message equating the magistrates with those mentioned in Psalm 2 who rebel against Christ.

Taufbüchlein

While the Anabaptist movement planted by Grebel was thus prospering, Zwingli was finishing and publishing his first book on baptism, titled *On Baptism, Rebaptism, and Infant Baptism*, usually known as the *Taufbüchlein* (*Little Baptism*

---

13   Johannes Kessler, *Sabbata*; from Harder, Leland, editor, *Sources of Swiss Anabaptism*, 1985, Herald Press, pp. 381-382. Used with permission.

Book). Having heard of the increasing strength of the Anabaptists in St. Gall, he dedicated the book to "the honorable, wise lords, burgomaster, councilmen, and the entire community of the city of St. Gallen".[14] In the book, he attempted to refute the Anabaptists and to build up his own understanding of baptism and infant baptism. He included the recently adopted liturgy of infant baptism used in Zürich and some brief excerpts from the debates held with the Anabaptists. As soon as the book was off the press, Zwingli sent several copies to Vadian in St. Gall.

Conrad Grebel, at the time still in Zürich, had also heard of the increasing success of the movement in his brother-in-law's home city. He had also heard of the St. Gall Council's increasing unrest and determination to do something regarding the movement, although no policy of persecution had yet been proposed or decided upon. (Indeed, St. Gall had not yet even officially embraced the Reformation.) Grebel knew that Vadian, as the beloved doctor and Reformer of the city, would have an immense influence upon the Council regarding what would or would not be done regarding the Anabaptist movement there.

With a heart surely filled with love, as well as his characteristic thorough-going zeal, Conrad Grebel wrote his last letter to his beloved friend and relative, Vadian. He began by expressing his deep appreciation for all that Vadian had done for him through his life, but yet he wanted in this letter to "be able to say to you what must be said, for. . . you have not been moved to give a ready ear more to the doctrine of the Spirit than to the doctrine of the flesh."[15] The message which he felt Vadian must hear was as follows:

---

14   Ulrich Zwingli, *On Baptism, Rebaptism, and Infant Baptism*, May 27, 1525; from Harder, Leland, editor, *Sources of Swiss Anabaptism*, 1985, Herald Press, p. 363. Used with permission.

15   Conrad Grebel to Vadian, May 30, 1525; from Harder, Leland, editor, *Sources of Swiss Anabaptism*, 1985, Herald Press, p. 378. Used with permission.

All or at least most of the blame is yours if anything is decreed against them [the Anabaptists of St. Gall] by way of prison, monetary fine, exile, or death. Beware, beware of innocent blood, for it is innocent. Whether you know it or do not know it, whether you wish it or do not wish it, it is innocent. Their suffering and the end of their lives and the great day of the Lord will prove it.... Let me say this, I beg, which is true in truth through Christ our Lord and Savior. The Lord permitting, I shall even unto death bear witness to the truth, in which they surely abide and you could (also). I know what is besetting you: money besets you, I think, or your knowledge of the flesh, or the unjust faction of Zwingli, the enemy of the truth in this matter. Do not destroy yourself, I beg. If you deceive men here, you will not escape notice before the presence of the Lord God, the knower of hearts and the just judge. Rather, turn away from the usury of money. Trust God, humble yourself, be content with little, turn away from the bloody faction of Zwingli, flee from your own to the divine wisdom so that you become a fool to the world but wise to the Lord. Become as a child, or you cannot enter into the kingdom of God.... If you do not want to stand with the brethren, at least do not resist them, so that you may be less blameworthy and an example of persecution is not given to other (city) states. I declare to you assuredly and truthfully by my faith in Christ, by heaven and earth and whatever

For the doctrine and precepts of the Lord are given in order to be fulfilled and put into practice.

~*Conrad Grebel to Vadian*

May I turn right?

If you were driving along a mountain road and encountered this sign, what would you immediately conclude?

You need to turn left, correct? But what if you did not want to go left? Could you argue that the sign does not forbid right turns? You could make such an argument, but a ditch or a cliff may settle your argument—and if a police officer is close enough to see you, you may have to argue with him as well.

This situation is similar to that existing in the discussions in Zürich. The Anabaptists were driving along the road and saw this sign. They turned left and concluded that turning right was forbidden. Zwingli was right behind them, but really wanted to get to a destination on his right, so he turned right, concluding that the sign did not forbid right turns.

The Anabaptists were saying, "The Scriptures command us to baptize believers; therefore, baptizing infants is forbidden." Zwingli was saying, "The Scriptures never explicitly forbid infant baptism, so we may do so." In his mind, since "he that believeth" does not *explicitly* exclude infants, infants could also be included. In the same way, since the sign above does not explicitly say, "Right turns illegal," he would conclude that they are permitted.

Using this analogy, the Anabaptists would have been correct. By warning that the road turns left, the sign indirectly forbids turning right—or continuing to go straight—at the peril of a disastrous wreck. Zwingli crashed his reformation by not heeding the warning signs.

Are we allowed to do whatever the Scriptures do not explicitly forbid? Yes, in the same sense that we are "permitted" to turn right when the road goes left. Drivers who live by this mindset will soon experience the jarring consequences of their folly!

is in them, that it is only from my love for you that I have admonished you in this way. Therefore I entreat you through Christ, do not despise me as I speak, warn from Christ, and take careful heed. . . . If you yield, I shall lay down my life for you. If you do not yield, I shall lay it down for those of our brethren against all who would oppose this truth. For I shall give testimony to the truth with the plundering of my goods and even of my house, which is all that I have. I shall give testimony with imprisonments, exiles, death, and the writing of a booklet, unless God should forbid. . . .

For the doctrine and precepts of the Lord are given in order to be fulfilled and put into practice.[16] Again I say, if you deceive the council, who do not give attention to this, you will not deceive the Lord.[17]

Repression in St. Gall

In St. Gall, the civil government was beginning to move to-wards repressing the Anabaptist movement. With about 800 members, the movement was growing stronger and stronger, and the government was not pleased. On May 12, they began to arrange a written exchange of views between the Zwinglians and the Anabaptists, requiring writings from both sides to be read before the Council. Neither side produced the required documents in time, but Vadian began to write a book against the Anabaptists,[18] and the local Anabaptists wrote to Conrad Grebel asking for a writing to defend their views.

---

16   This sentence could probably be taken to sum up the essence of early Anabaptism.

17   Conrad Grebel to Vadian, May 30, 1525; from Harder, Leland, editor, *Sources of Swiss Anabaptism*, 1985, Herald Press, pp. 378-380. Used with permission.

18   Unfortunately no longer extant. Kessler gives this summary of its contents: "how the manner and practice of preaching of the Anabaptists was an improper misdemeanor against the custom and teaching of the apostles and undertaken by their own choice without any Christian calling; and he would

The interior of the chapel in St. Gall where the Anabaptists sat in the balcony, listening to the reading of Zwingli's book promoting infant baptism. Gabriel Giger called out from the balcony, "Stop reading and give us God's Word instead of Zwingli's!"

The exchange of views had not yet taken place when one of the Zwinglian preachers in St. Gall by the name of Dominic Zili read Zwingli's *Taufbüchlein* and was very impressed—so much so, in fact, that he offered to read the entire book to his congregation in a Sunday evening service. He also wanted the Anabaptists to come and reply to the book with Scripture.

That evening, Zili faced his own congregants as well as the council and the burgomaster, who had come to hear the reading of Zwingli's book. Several Anabaptist leaders who had been invited also came and sat in the balcony at the back of the church building. Just as Zili raised Zwingli's book to begin reading from it, Gabriel Giger[19]—an Anabaptist leader who was sitting in the balcony—cried out, "Oh, I am sorry that the poor people present here are to be misled by such a book.

---

base it on Scripture." Johannes Kessler, "The Reactions to Anabaptism in St. Gallen"; from Harder, Leland, editor, *Sources of Swiss Anabaptism*, 1985, Herald Press, p. 383. Used with permission.

19   Giger may have been baptized on January 21, 1525, the night of the very first Anabaptist baptism. In any case, he was baptized by Conrad Grebel in Felix Manz's house.

Stop reading and give us God's Word instead of Zwingli's."[20] St. Gall chronicler Johannes Kessler later reported, "By these words they [the Anabaptists] won over the assembly. The people regarded them as if the truth of God were with them, but they regarded Dominic as if he were giving the doctrine of men."[21] Zili continued to say, "Dear brethren, these are not Zwingli's and not man's words, but founded on God's Word."[22] The crowd nevertheless insisted that Zwingli's book be laid aside as man's word. The following conversation (reported by Kessler) ensued:

> In this tension the burgomaster began to speak … "Dominic, you are to read the book, and they are to reply to the arguments and Scriptures." Then another Anabaptist said: "We are awaiting also for a writing by Brother Conrad Grebel. When we get it, we will give answer." Thereupon the burgomaster said, "Since you could speak so happily at the Shooting Lodge[23] without Grebel, do it here too." They replied again, "We have a letter here from Conrad Grebel to the burgomaster and the council. We want to read it, so listen carefully to what C. Grebel has to offer against Zwingli." The burgomaster said: "If you have kept letters from us, why do you not give them to us? You should hand them to us and not read them."[24]

After much more discussion, the Anabaptists left the balcony saying: "If you have Zwingli's word, we want to have God's Word."[25]

---

20 Johannes Kessler, *Sabbata*; from Harder, Leland, editor, *Sources of Swiss Anabaptism*, 1985, Herald Press, p. 383. Used with permission.
21 *Ibid.*
22 *Ibid.*
23 A location where the Anabaptists held meetings.
24 Johannes Kessler, *Sabbata*; from Harder, Leland, editor, *Sources of Swiss Anabaptism*, 1985, Herald Press, pp. 383-384. Used with permission.
25 *Ibid.*, p. 384.

Balthasar Hubmaier was a theologian who accepted believer's baptism. However, he did not reject the union of church and state, and tried to make an Anabaptist State Church. So while technically he was an Anabaptist, by accepting rebaptism, he was not of the same spirit as Conrad Grebel and those who practiced nonresistance.

Following this disturbance in the St. Lawrence Cathedral, the Council held their planned exchange of views on June 5, 1525. Grebel's letter to the Council and burgomaster was read first, then Vadian read his book against the Anabaptists. Vadian had finally made up his mind and come out against the Anabaptists, never (as far as we know) to change his mind. The Anabaptists were given an opportunity to read a reply that had been written (perhaps by Grebel) to Vadian's book. The Council decided to suppress the Anabaptist movement, imposing a sentence of banishment on anyone who would rebaptize or hold the Lord's Supper outside the state church within the territory of St. Gall. However, the Anabaptists would be allowed to meet in St. Lawrence's Cathedral at stated times. The Council also commissioned a force of 200 men to handle any rebellion which might break out. Sadly, the Anabaptist leaders were soon banished from the canton, and the movement in St. Gall shrank and went underground. Without Scriptural leadership, some Anabaptists degraded into practicing bizarre and repulsive behaviors, which gave the Zwinglians a handy excuse for further persecution and suppression of Anabaptism elsewhere in Switzerland.[26]

In the meantime, Zwingli wrote yet another anti-Anabaptist tract, titled *Concerning the Office of Preaching*. He felt that the itinerant Anabaptist missionaries did not have a legitimate commission to preach, and wrote against their preaching.

Waldshut

In early June, Conrad Grebel took to the road once more, leaving Zürich to visit Waldshut in southern Germany at the invitation of Balthasar Hubmaier. Hubmaier had been a Zwinglian leader of the congregation at Waldshut, leading the way of reform there. He and most of his congregation had been baptized by Wilhelm Reublin, and Hubmaier was now working on a book regarding believer's baptism.

Accompanied by fellow-Anabaptist Jakob Hottinger, Conrad traveled to Waldshut where the two visited with Hubmaier and discussed baptism. We do not know what other subjects may have been discussed by them. While Hubmaier was an articulate and able defender of believer's baptism and some other scriptural beliefs and practices, such as church discipline, he never embraced nonresistance, nor did he come to the realization that church and state must be separate. He clung to the state church model to the end. His relationship to Grebel and his group has been the subject of much discussion, but it seems clear that Hubmaier and Grebel would at least have disagreed on the subject of nonresistance.

---

26   See John Horsch, "Inquiry into the truth of accusations of fanaticism and crime against the early Swiss Brethren," *Mennonite Quarterly Review* 8(1) (January 1934):18-31 and 8(2) (April 1934):73-89; Harder, Leland, editor, *Sources of Swiss Anabaptism*, 1985, Herald Press, pp. 455-456; C. Arnold Snyder, "The Birth and Evolution of Swiss Anabaptism, 1520-1530," *Mennonite Quarterly Review* 80(4) (October 2006):501-645.

Grüningen

After his visit to Hubmaier in Waldshut, Grebel went to the region southeast of Zürich to work in the vicinity of Grüningen. Conrad's father had been magistrate in Grüningen for 12 years while Conrad was a boy. The Grüningen peasants, as well as some of the pastors, had been quite insistent earlier in the Reformation on the abolition of the tithes. However, the central government in Zürich had forced the tithe upon them. The peasants were also advocating the local selection of pastors. This was also not granted. These grievances gave them a listening ear when Conrad Grebel showed up—a man who also openly stated that he had not received justice from Zürich.

With aid from some of the Brethren from Zollikon, such as Marx Bosshart, Grebel began a time of most successful evangelization and missionary work. He found an enthusiastic audience with the peasants, and he was even successful in getting most of the local Zwinglian pastors to admit that infant baptism could not be defended from the Scriptures. More than one confessed that if he did not fear the Zürich government or anyone else, he would not continue to baptize infants. One pastor, after debating the subject of baptism with Grebel, finally said: "Milords have issued a mandate; I will stick to it." (In other words, he would continue baptizing infants because the government had ordered it.) To this, Grebel replied, "Are you a man? You should not regard Milords or anyone else and should do only what God has commanded and follow after what the mouth of God has spoken."[27] Grebel also said that if he were imprisoned, he would ask only that he be given pen and ink, and then, even though he could not be heard, he would at least be heard through his writings. He would then ask that he and Zwingli could have a debate, and

---

27   Court Testimony in Grüningen, July 12, 1525; from Harder, Leland, editor, *Sources of Swiss Anabaptism*, 1985, Herald Press, p. 421. Used with permission.

if he (Grebel) was found to be in error, he would be willing to be burned at the stake. If Zwingli was shown to be in error, however, then he would not ask that Zwingli be burnt.

Grebel's mission to the Grüningen neighborhood began in June, 1525. By early July, the Zürich government had gotten wind of Grebel's activities, and was not pleased. Some of the things which Grebel and Bosshart had said about Zwingli and his *Taufbüchlein* were denied by Zwingli, and the Zürich government called the two to come to Zürich and answer for their statements. For instance, Bosshart was accused of saying that in the *Taufbüchlein*, "Zwingli has written plain lies."[28]

In response to the summons, Grebel and Bosshart wrote a letter to the Zürich Council, requesting a safe conduct to and from the hearing. This was a guarantee that they would not be harmed or arrested, and would be allowed to safely return after the hearing. The Council did not grant the request, and Grebel decided not to go. Bosshart, however, went, along with two other Anabaptists—and they were promptly arrested and thrown into prison. Bosshart remained there for nearly a month, until he promised to cease preaching and baptizing and was fined. In the meantime, Grebel was still free and went on to the immediate vicinity of the town of Grüningen.

While he was in Grüningen, or perhaps earlier, Grebel wrote a Bible concordance collecting Scripture references under two headings: 1) "Concerning the faith of God, which must come from heaven alone and through whom we are saved and thereafter baptized"; and 2) "The true and thorough Word of God concerning baptism." It is believed that Grebel was the compiler of this document, which he gave to another Anabaptist who later published it under his own name.

---

28   Harold S. Bender, *Conrad Grebel 1498-1526: Founder of the Swiss Brethren*, 1950, Mennonite Historical Society, p. 149.

Coming Persecution

Grebel had long expected persecution at the hands of Zürich. Although he himself had not yet been imprisoned, Blaurock and Manz had both sat in Zürich jails, as had many of their converts. Grebel undoubtedly knew that his successful, peaceful days in Grüningen could not last forever.

Nevertheless, sometime probably in October, 1525, Blaurock and Manz arrived in Grüningen to aid in preaching with Grebel. The three brethren may not have realized how close persecution was.

6

Triumph Under Persecution

rüningen bailiff Jörg Berger wrote to the Zürich Council, "We had an extraordinary day!" That Sunday morning, October 8, 1525, in the parish church of Hinwil in the territory of Grüningen, Georg Blaurock had walked in before the pastor had arrived. Blaurock boldly mounted the pulpit and asked, "Whose place is this? If this is the place of God where the Word of God is proclaimed, then I am a messenger from the Father to proclaim the Word of God."[1]

Following this, Blaurock began to preach to an audience of about 200 people. The local pastor arrived, and was no doubt surprised to find an Anabaptist in his pulpit. He listened to Blaurock's sermon until Blaurock began to speak about baptism. At this, the pastor interrupted from the audience. The people began to murmur at this, and finally the pastor began shouting for order and left. The deputy bailiff, who was present, then tried to arrest Blaurock, but the congregation challenged him, asking if he had been ordered to do so. Since

---

1   Jörg Berger to the Zürich Council, October 8, 1525; from Harder, Leland, editor, *Sources of Swiss Anabaptism*, 1985, Herald Press, p. 430. Used with permission.

Anabaptists being hunted in the Grüningen woods.

he had received no such order, he left with three other men to get Bailiff Berger.

Berger arrived with the deputy bailiff and his own servant. He spoke some to the people, and then began to debate Blaurock. "It seemed to me he did not want to be seized," Berger later commented.[2] Finally he placed Blaurock under arrest, mounted his servant's horse, and left. A great crowd followed Blaurock.

Berger had heard of Anabaptists in another nearby town who wanted to hold a meeting, so he went there with his prisoner and admonished them to cease baptizing. They replied that they would not force anyone, but that if anyone desired baptism, they would baptize. The meeting was held as planned, with Conrad Grebel and Felix Manz (who had been released from prison in Zürich the previous day) officiating. Berger recognized Grebel and Manz, and quickly consulted with his servant and deputy. Having come to a decision as to what to do, Berger went to a nearby town, gathered as many men as he could, and sent them back to the deputy bailiff in hopes of arresting the two leaders. Berger himself rode on to the

_____
2   *Ibid.*, p. 430.

Grüningen castle with Blaurock. The deputy and his men arrested Conrad Grebel, but Felix Manz escaped.

The day ended with Georg Blaurock and Conrad Grebel sitting in the dungeon of the castle where Conrad had lived as a boy, and Bailiff Berger writing a letter about the events to the Zürich Council. "We had an extraordinary day," he said. When Zwingli heard the news, he wrote to Vadian:

> Conrad Grebel together with Jörg, that man of fickle mind, has been arrested at Grüningen and thrown into prison. Inclined toward evil signs by nature, he [Grebel] has always sought some tragedy. Now he has found it. May Almighty God grant that his Word may not be violated, for some fathers-in-law are such that I would assign not only too little hope to them but even too little faith.[3]

Zwingli's evident satisfaction at Grebel and Blaurock's arrest was tempered by his apprehension over the reaction of Jacob Grebel. Senator Grebel did not always go along with Zwingli's program, and Zwingli suspected Grebel of being secretly loyal to Catholicism.

Third Disputation

Three weeks after Grebel and Blaurock were arrested, the Zürich authorities caught up with Felix Manz and arrested him as well. With the three leaders sitting in jail, the authorities in Grüningen—Bailiff Berger and the Twelve Judges—officially requested that Zürich host yet another public disputation on baptism. They thought this would be an excellent way to help suppress the movement. Balthasar Hubmaier was also requesting a disputation with Zwingli. The Zürich authorities, possibly motivated by the publication of Balthasar Hubmaier's

---

3   Ulrich Zwingli to Vadian, October 11, 1525; from Harder, Leland, editor, *Sources of Swiss Anabaptism*, 1985, Herald Press, pp. 431-432. Used with permission.

The November, 1525, disputation with the Anabaptists. So many people showed up that the meeting had to be held in the Grossmünster chapel, rather than the city council house.

Taufbüchlein, which was now circulating through Switzerland, agreed to host another disputation. The Anabaptists were also saying that although there had been disputations before, they had not been fair, as Zwingli had not allowed them to speak their minds. Accordingly, the disputation opened on November 6, 1525, with the rule that the platform would be open to anything anyone thought could be supported by Scripture.

The disputation lasted for three days—November 6-8, 1525. Among those presiding over the disputation were Vadian and Sebastian Hofmeister, who had once been so close to becoming an Anabaptist himself. Although Hubmaier wanted to attend, he was unable to due to the Austrian troops about to occupy his "rebellious" Protestant/Anabaptist city of Waldshut. Instead of Hubmaier, Grebel, Manz, and Blaurock were brought from prison to represent the Anabaptists. The disputation was to be held in the *Rathaus* (Council House), but so many people came—Zwinglians and Anabaptists, government personnel and peasants—that the debate was moved to the Grossmünster cathedral. Once again, no official minutes were taken for the disputation, and the Zwinglians claimed victory for themselves.

Following the disputation, the Anabaptists were immediately placed on trial—a trial which lasted, off and on, from November 9-18. As to be expected, Ulrich Zwingli was one of the foremost witnesses on behalf of the state against the Anabaptists, but the second witness was none other than Sebastian Hofmeister—who earlier had nearly converted to Anabaptism. Now he was accusing the Anabaptists in court. The accusations were wide-ranging, and ran the gamut from the standard charges (that they wanted to establish a special, separate church, that they wanted to abolish the government, that they slandered Zwingli, etc.) to what seems now as very strange grounds for a state accusation (for instance, Zwingli accused Grebel of having "said at the disputation on Monday that he thought the Messiah might be already present, but it is not known what or whom he meant thereby."[4]).

> *Whoever is a coveter, usurer, gambler, or the like should never be [included] among Christians, but be excluded by the ban, as taught in Scripture....*
>
> ~Conrad Grebel

Conrad Grebel's recorded testimony reads, in part, as follows:

> Conrad Grebel persists that infant baptism is of the devil and rebaptism is right and that Zwingli is teaching falsely and wrongly.
>
> Next, he does not admit that he ever taught that one should have to give his property to anybody for nothing.

---

4 "The Trial of Grebel, Mantz, and Blaurock," between November 9 and 18, 1525; from Harder, Leland, editor, *Sources of Swiss Anabaptism*, 1985, Herald Press, p. 438. Used with permission.

Concerning the church he said that whoever is a coveter, usurer, gambler, or the like should never be [included] among Christians but be excluded by the ban, as taught in Scripture....

Nor did he ever teach that one should not be obedient to the authorities ... he had never said to him [Hofmeister] that government should be abolished.[5]

Blaurock submitted a written statement to the Council, which said:

I am a door, he who enters through me finds pasture but he who enters elsewhere is a thief and a murderer, as it is written. I am a good shepherd. A good shepherd gives his soul for the sheep. Thus I too offer my body and life and soul for my sheep, my body in the Tower, my life in the sword, or fire, or in the winepress have my blood pressed from my flesh like Christ on the cross. I am a beginner of the baptism of Christ and the bread of the Lord together with my elect brethren in Christ, Conrad Grebel and Felix Mantz. On this account the pope with his following is a thief and a murderer, Luther is a thief and a murderer with his following, and Zwingli and Leo Jud are thieves and murderers of Christ with their following until they acknowledge this. I have desired and still desire of my gracious Lords of Zurich to debate with Huldrych Zwingli and Leo Jud, and am unable to get it. But I am waiting for the hour that my heavenly Father has ordained for it.[6]

Felix Manz's testimony reads, in part:

Felix Mantz gives his answer that the Scriptures and their bases are so firm that they cannot be set aside or overcome, so therefore infant baptism is wrong and

---

5   *Ibid.*, p. 439.
6   *Ibid.*, p. 440.

rebaptism right; and since Zwingli teaches it, he teaches wrongly and falsely.

And so nothing has impelled him to deny infant baptism and to oppose it but the clear and true Scriptures. And so also nothing else led him to rebaptism but that he knew well that he had not been baptized....

Concerning government he said no Christian strikes with the sword, nor does he resist evil.[7]

At the end of the trial, the Council passed the following sentence on the three Anabaptist leaders:

> Inasmuch as Conrad Grebel, Felix Mantz, and Jörg of the House of Jacob were imprisoned by Milords because of their rebaptism and improper conduct, etc., it is declared that all three are to be put together into the New Tower and fed on bread, mush, and water. No one is to visit them or depart from them except the prescribed attendants, as long as God pleases and it seems good to Milords, etc.[8]

Margaret Hottinger, another Anabaptist who had been arrested, was also imprisoned in the tower with the three leaders. Also in this sentence is the first known reference to Michael Sattler, who had apparently been arrested by the Zürich authorities on suspicion of Anabaptism. He was released upon paying the costs of his imprisonment and swearing never to return to Zürich. It is believed that he had not yet been rebaptized.[9]

In addition to the sentence, the Zürich Council issued yet another mandate against Anabaptism which it sent to the magistrates at Grüningen. It stated that "In the debate held in the city hall and the Grossmünster ... infant baptism was shown to be biblical. And because of this, it is our prohibition and serious judgment that henceforth everyone—men and women,

---

7   *Ibid.*, pp. 441-442.
8   *Ibid.*, p. 442.
9   This is the same man who would later be the main author of the Schleitheim Confession.

boys and girls abstain from all rebaptism, no longer practice it, but baptize the infants. For whoever acts to the contrary, whenever it occurs, shall be fined a silver mark."[10]

On Trial Again

About four months later, the three Anabaptist leaders were put on trial once again, with several other Anabaptists who had been arrested by the Zürich authorities. They had even managed to arrest Balthasar Hubmaier, who had fled to Switzerland from Waldshut, which had fallen to King Ferdinand's Catholic troops. They imprisoned him in solitary confinement and tortured him on the rack to try to get him to recant. The re-trial ran from March 5-7, 1526. The three leaders' testimonies were recorded as follows:

> Felix Mantz answers: you will and you must learn that infant baptism is not right and not Christ's baptism. You have not permitted me to write as I always hoped you would because you kept me in prison. I did not argue but witnessed to my faith. I shall confess it to the end in the power of him who will strengthen me with his truth. Concerning other things and charges of your law, I will answer as truly as is right.
>
> Jörg Blaurock's answer is that he will stay by the baptism of Christ which he has accepted, and all those who baptize infants are murderers and thieves against God. And if they want many answers, let them read the letter that he wrote to the preachers in the churches. He will stay with that until death.
>
> Conrad Grebel answers and persists in the belief that infant baptism is wrong and the baptism he accepted is right. He will stay by that and let God rule. He would

---

10   "Mandate of the Zürich Council to the Grüningen Magistrates," November 30, 1525; from Harder, Leland, editor, *Sources of Swiss Anabaptism*, 1985, Herald Press, p. 443. Used with permission.

otherwise be obedient to Milords in all other secular matters. He also hopes to show that Zwingli errs in these and other things, and also asks Milords to permit him to write, like Zwingli. Then he can prove it. If he fails to do so, he is willing to suffer whatever God wills.[11]

Following the trial, eighteen Anabaptists were sentenced as follows:

Concerning these Anabaptists, it is declared that upon their answers which each one gave and their opinions persisted in, that they shall be put together into the New Tower; and they shall be given nothing to eat but bread and water and bedded on straw. And the attendant who guards them shall under oath let no one come to them or go away from them. Thus let them die in the Tower unless anyone desists from his acts and error and intends to be obedient. That should then be brought to [the attention of] Milords' councilors and representatives. And then they shall be asked how further to punish them. No one shall have the authority to alter their confinement, behind the backs of said Milords, whether they are sick or well.

Similarly, the girls and women shall be placed together and treated in every respect as stated above.[12]

They also issued another anti-Anabaptist mandate:

Inasmuch as Our Lords, burgomaster, [Small] Council, and Large Council, which are called the Two Hundred of the city of Zurich, have for some time earnestly endeavored to turn the deceived, mistaken Anabaptists from their error, etc., but inasmuch as some of them,

---

11   Retrial of the Anabaptists, March 5-7, 1526; from Harder, Leland, editor, *Sources of Swiss Anabaptism*, 1985, Herald Press, p. 444. Used with permission.

12   "The Tenth Disputation with the Anabaptists: Their Retrial and Sentencing," March 5-7, 1526; from Harder, Leland, editor, *Sources of Swiss Anabaptism*, 1985, Herald Press, p. 447. Used with permission.

An artist's conception of an Anabaptist escape from a tower prison dungeon.

hardened against their oaths, vows, and pledges, have shown disobedience to the injury of public order and authority and the subversion of the common interest and true Christian conduct, some of them—men, women, and girls were sentenced by Our Lords to severe punishment and imprisonment. And it is therefore the earnest command, order, and warning of the said Our Lords that no one in their city, country, and domain, whether man, woman, or girl, shall henceforth baptize another. Whoever henceforth baptizes another will be seized by Our Lords and, according to this present explicit decree, drowned without any mercy. Hereafter, everyone knows how to avoid this so that no one gives cause for his own death.[13]

For the first time, the Zürich authorities had ordered the death penalty for Anabaptism.

---

13   *Ibid.*, p. 448.

Zwingli wrote to Vadian, who was now the burgomaster of St. Gall:

> This day, most honorable burgomaster, it has been decreed by the Council of Two Hundred that the Anabaptist ringleaders shall be cast back into the Tower in which they previously lay [and] enticed by bread and water until they either die or surrender. It was further decided that whoever is baptized hereafter will be submerged permanently. This decision has already been proclaimed. Thus patience has endured enough and finally erupted. Your father-in-law senator implored mercy in vain. The incorrigibly impetuous audacity of these people first pains and then irks me.[14]

Escape!

So the Anabaptists sat in the prison tower, under a sentence of life imprisonment.

It was to prove to be a very short life imprisonment.

The Anabaptists were in the tower for a couple of weeks. They had managed to bring in Bibles, a flint and steel, and some wax candles. During that time, Grebel, Manz, and Blaurock were reading and encouraging the others. They were all determined to die for their faith, and expected to do so in the Tower.

However, one stormy night—March 21, 1526—things took a different turn. The guard had brought them their water, and they were drinking and eating some bread when one of the prisoners mentioned something that all of them had already noticed—there was a window shutter which looked loose enough to move. Unspoken was the implication that they might be able to escape through it. At first, the prisoners did not pay much

---

14   Ulrich Zwingli to Vadian, on or after March 7, 1526; from Harder, Leland, editor, *Sources of Swiss Anabaptism*, 1985, Herald Press, p. 449. Used with permission.

attention to the suggestion. They were resigned to death in the Tower. However, another loose shutter down lower in the Tower was noticed, and one of the prisoners broke it off to use for a pry. They pushed at the upper shutter, and sure enough, it moved. One of the Anabaptists found a way to climb up to the shutter and was able to prop it open with books and blocks of wood, far enough for a man to crawl through. Felix Manz climbed up, then another Anabaptist.

Using the rope which had lowered them all into the tower, the three by the shutter pulled up the man who had pointed out the loose shutter in the first place. From this vantage point, the four began discussing their options. They could easily get out—but they had seen the drawbridge shut and the gate locked, someone objected. Then it was pointed out that, no, everything was open outside. (Even the moat underneath the Tower was dry at the time.) Then one of the prisoners began begging the four to take him out of the Tower, for he could not survive there. After this, the four set to work. Using their rope, they were able to pull the prisoners up, one by one, from the floor of the cell to the window. They were then able to use the same rope to let them down out of the Tower into the (dry) moat.

Once they were all out of the Tower and standing in the moat, they began discussing where they should go. It was jok-ingly suggested that they should go across the sea, to the red Indians.[15] After they had made and discussed their plans, they went up to the guard. He just so happened to be the brother of one of the prisoners, and he let them out. He even harbored one or two of the escaped prisoners in his house for the night. All of them were able to get away from the Zürich authorities except two, who were too sick or weak to escape recapture.

---

15   As humorous as this suggestion may have sounded to the tiny group in the moat that stormy night in 1526, they probably could not have imagined that hundreds of years later, there would be tens of thousands of Anabaptists living in religious freedom "across the sea" in the land of the red Indians.

Conrad died of the plague in Maienfeld, the town in the background left of this photo. Maienfeld was the setting of the popular children's book Heidi, *written in the 1800s.*

They were arrested, put on trial again, and were banished from Zürich with the threat of execution if they ever returned.

Final Mission

Grebel's whereabouts and activities for the final five or so months of his life following his prison escape are not known with certainty. Fleeing the "justice" of Zürich, he did not want to divulge his destination to those who met him. It was during these months that he most likely wrote a small booklet against Zwingli's books regarding infant baptism. This small booklet was circulated among the Swiss Brethren, possibly in printed form, and Zwingli was finally able to obtain a copy and wrote against it in 1527.

In the meantime, harsh persecution and lack of adequate, Scriptural leadership were taking their toll among some Anabaptists. In some places, what had once been solid Anabaptist congregations begun by the missionary labors of Manz and

Grebel were descending into bizarre forms of behavior. Manz and Grebel, grieved by this, tried to correct the imbalances which they saw in places such as Appenzell, where it is believed that Grebel went to preach. Some of these "Anabaptists," however, lashed out at Manz and Grebel, calling them false prophets and scribes.

After his mission in Appenzell, where he may have worked together with Felix Manz, Grebel is reported to have traveled to the town of Maienfeld. His older sister, Barbara, may have been living there at the time; the Anabaptist movement had also reached the town previously. He may have wanted to visit the Brethren, or his sister, or both. It is also possible that he wanted to rest. The long stay in the prison tower in Zürich no doubt took a severe toll on his health. The plague was raging in Appenzell at the time. Worn out by lifelong disease, long imprisonment, and controversy, Conrad Grebel arrived in Maienfeld. It was to be the end of his final missionary journey. Around August, 1526, Conrad Grebel died in Maienfeld of the plague.

Afterward

Although Grebel was gone, his influence lived on, and still lives on to this day. The story did not end with his death.

Ulrich Zwingli was not ready to give up his fight against the Anabaptists—even though his archenemy, Conrad Grebel, had eluded his grasp. Although the death penalty had been decreed against them, there was resistance to this stance in the Zürich Council. This resistance was led by none other than Jacob Grebel. To make matters worse, Zwingli was convinced that Grebel and several others on the Council had been bribed by the Catholic cantons, and were acting to the detriment of the Reformation. This man had to go if Zwingli was to have his way.

This memorial marks the location where Felix Manz was drowned in the Limmat River. The Grossmünster towers rise in the background. The memorial also mentions Hans Landis, an Anabaptist who was martyred here almost a century later.

In pursuance of this goal, Zwingli began gathering evidence for what he considered illegal taking of foreign pensions (in the form of Conrad's scholarships) by Jacob Grebel. He considered this unpatriotic and illegal. He preached against such activity from the pulpit, stirring up public sentiment against such activity, then brought charges against Jacob Grebel. This was done before a secret council that had been set up, and Zwingli admitted to forming a "dictatorship." At the trial of Jacob Grebel, his financial deeds and misdeeds going years back were brought up, including his pocketing of money which he was supposed to have forwarded to Conrad for foreign scholarships, and his failure to give this money to Conrad's wife upon his death. Grebel was found guilty and sentenced to death. This was a shock, as nothing Jacob had done was considered by most to be worthy of death. The sentence was very hastily carried out, with Jacob protesting all the way that he did not deserve this. It was the sentiment of most of the people of Zürich that if the sentence had not been so speedily carried out, nothing would have happened to Grebel.

But at the end of the day, Zwingli reigned nearly supreme in Zürich. No one now would dare to defy his authority—no one, that is, except the Anabaptists. Felix Manz and Georg Blaurock returned to Grüningen to continue their mission there. They were arrested by Bailiff Berger and sent to Zürich for trial and sentencing. On January 5, 1527, Felix Manz was sentenced to death:

> because contrary to Christian order and custom he had become involved in Anabaptism, had accepted it, taught others, and become a leader and beginner of these things because he confessed having said that he wanted to gather those who wanted to accept Christ and follow Him, and unite himself with them through baptism, and let the rest live according to their faith, so that he and his followers separated themselves from the Christian Church and were about to raise up and prepare a sect of their own under

For all they that take the sword shall perish with the sword. Mt. 26:52

These words of Jesus came true for Zwingli, pictured here dying on the battlefield. His body was taken by the victorious Catholics and burned as a heretic. Dying with him in the battle were another 24 Protestant pastors and a couple of ex-Anabaptists.

The photo below, taken from the photo on pages 8-9 (upper middle), shows the approximate location of the battlefield where Zwingli died.

the guise of a Christian meeting and church; because he had condemned capital punishment, and in order to increase his following had boasted of certain revelations from the Pauline Epistles. But since such doctrine is harmful to the unified usage of all Christendom, and leads to offense, insurrection, and sedition against the government, to the shattering of the common peace, brotherly love, and civil cooperation and to all evil, Manz shall be delivered to the executioner, who shall tie his hands, put him into a boat, take him to the lower hut, there strip his bound hands down over his knees, place a stick between his knees and arms, and thus push him into the water and let him perish in the water; thereby he shall have atoned to the law and justice.... His property shall also be confiscated by my lords.[16]

As he was being led from the prison to the place of execution, Manz cheerfully told the people that he was going to die for the truth. He praised GOD with a loud voice. He hardly listened to the Zwinglian preacher at his side, who was trying to convince him to recant. Yet he did hear his mother on the shore, loudly calling for him to be steadfast. As he was being bound, he sang in a loud voice in Latin, "Into Thy Hands, Lord, I commend my spirit." He was then pushed under the crystal-clear waters of the Limmat River, drowned, then buried in the St. Jakob's Cemetery in Zürich.

Blaurock, because no evidence had been presented that he had baptized in Zürich following the March 7 mandate, and because he had not previously sworn an oath to desist from baptizing and leave Zürich, was not executed. His sentence reads, in part, as follows:

Georg vom Hause Jakob, called Blaurock, who as a true instigator and chief agent of Anabaptism has previously

---

16   Christian Neff & Harold S. Bender, "Manz, Felix," in Krahn, Cornelius, editor, *Mennonite Encyclopedia*, Vol. 3. 1955, 1985, Herald Press, p. 473. Used with permission.

Conrad's posterity

Following Conrad's death, Barbara remarried a Zürich citizen by the name of Jacob Ziegler. Conrad's daughter Rachel seems to have died in infancy; his oldest son, Theophil, died about 1541, unmarried. Conrad's son Joshua was the only one of his children to marry, and he had three sons and four daughters. One of these sons, also named Conrad, was the Zürich city treasurer in 1624. He may have participated in the trial and prosecution of Hans Landis, the last Anabaptist sentenced to death in Switzerland, in 1614. Another descendant was burgomaster of Zürich; other descendants served in other prominent positions. Thirteen generations later, one of Conrad's direct descendants, Dean Hans Rudolf von Grebel, was pastor at the Grossmünster chapel.

Conrad was a new convert, having been a serious Christian for only a few short years. He had not married while in the faith, and his family suffered from his decision. Some of the later Swiss Brethren can now count 18 generations of descendants, some of whom still cling to following Christ in a way that would most likely cause Conrad to rejoice.

been held in the dungeon of my lords and in hope of future improvement and that he would cease his erroneous plan of Anabaptism was graciously released, since his mere word was accepted without an oath as he wished it, yet he disregarded this; and although it was told him in clear words that if he ever returned into the realm and territory of our lords he would receive the penalty he deserved, he has nevertheless come back, and, even though he says he has not baptized since then, he has accused the preachers of doing violence to and falsifying Scripture in spite of the disputations, whereas rebaptism is altogether in opposition to and prejudicial to the Scripture as well as to common good usage, which has been preserved unanimously throughout all Christendom, and (rebaptism) has thus far created only offense and insurrection, he should for this seditious character, meeting in mobs and misconduct against Christian government and Christian authority be mercifully sentenced thus; the executioner shall be ordered to remove his clothing to the waist, tie his hands, and then beat him with rods from the Fish Market down the street to the gate in Niederdorf ... he is then to be banished under oath, the penalty for return being death by drowning.[17]

The sentence was carried out on the same day as Felix Manz's execution. Blaurock nearly died from the cruel treatment. When they reached the gate, they forced Blaurock to swear an oath to never return on threat of further imprisonment. Following this official banishment, Blaurock took his shoes and shook the dust from them over the city.

Following the banishment of Blaurock and the execution of Manz, Zwingli's power in Zürich grew and grew. But the Anabaptist movement did not stop—rather, it became more unified and grew. When Zwingli finally got his hands on a copy of Grebel's *Confutation* of his arguments in favor of infant baptism, he wrote his final book against the Anabaptists, the *Refutation of the Tricks of the Catabaptists*. The book contained an account of Zwingli's view of Anabaptist beginnings and history, as well as his reply to Grebel's booklet and the Schleitheim Confession. But while Zwingli was done writing against the Anabaptists, he was not done persecuting them. More executions followed Manz's in Zürich, and in September, 1527, with Zwingli's help, the Reformed cantons of Zürich, Bern, and St. Gall issued a joint edict of persecution against the Anabaptists. It ordered a program of admonition for suspected Anabaptists, punishment for those who refused to recant, banishment for foreign Anabaptists found within the three territories, and drowning for returning Anabaptists

17   Christian Neff, "Blaurock (Cajacob), Georg," in Krahn, Cornelius, editor, Mennonite Encyclopedia, Vol. 1. 1955, 1983, Herald Press, p. 358. Used with permission.

The city authorities found no legal reason to execute Georg Blaurock, so they whipped him out of town. When he reached the city gate, George literally shook the dust off his feet over the city.

or for teachers who had promised to cease teaching but had continued anyway.

In 1531, Zwingli met a premature end on the battlefield in the Second Kappel War. He was not a combatant in the war—he was serving as a chaplain. However, his violence and approval of violence had finally come home, and as Jesus said, the man who had taken the sword died by it at last. Upon hearing of Zwingli's death, a tearful Vadian wrote in his diary, "with this punishment God has clearly indicated that servants of the Word should not conform themselves to war but to peace and its teaching."[18]

With Grebel and Manz dead and Blaurock traveling far away, the Swiss Brethren movement threatened to disintegrate into doctrinal error, fanaticism, bizarre behavior, and finally nonexistence. However, God raised up another man who, with his leadership abilities, writing skills, doctrinal discernment, and advantageous placement in the kingdom of God at the right place and time, is credited with keeping that from happening. That man was Michael Sattler, one of the second wave of early Swiss Brethren leaders. His life is another story....

18   As cited by Harder, Leland, editor, *Sources of Swiss Anabaptism*, 1985, Herald Press, p. 461. Used with permission.

Bibliography

Baylor, Michael, Gerald Biesecker-Mast, Geoffrey Dipple, Thomas Finger, Abraham Friesen, Ray Gingerich, Hans-Jürgen Goertz, H.W. Walker Pipkin, & J. Denny Weaver. "Responses to Snyder's 'The Birth and Evolution of Swiss Anabaptism,'" *Mennonite Quarterly Review* 80(4) (October 2006):647-690.

Bender, Harold S., *Conrad Grebel 1498-1526*, 1950, Mennonite Historical Society.

Blanke, Fritz, *Brothers in Christ*, 1961, Herald Press.

Catechism of the Catholic Church, 1994, Liguri Publications.

Friesen, Abraham, *Reformers, Radicals, Revolutionaries*, 2012, Institute for Mennonite Studies.

Furcha, E. J., editor, *The Essential Carlstadt*, 1995, Herald Press.

Harder, Leland, editor, *The Sources of Swiss Anabaptism*, 1985, Herald Press.

Hillerbrand, Hans J., *The World of the Reformation*, 1973, Baker Book House.

Krahn, Cornelius, editor, *Mennonite Encyclopedia*, 4 volumes, 1955-1959, Herald Press.

Pries, Edmund, "Oath Refusal in Zurich from 1525 to 1527: The Erratic Emergence of Anabaptist Practice," in Walter Klaassen, editor, *Anabaptism Revisited*, 1992, Herald Press.

Ruth, John L., *Conrad Grebel Son of Zurich*, 1975, Herald Press.

Sider, Ronald J., editor, *Karlstadt's Battle with Luther*, 1978, Fortress Press.

Snyder, C. Arnold, "The Birth and Evolution of Swiss Anabaptism, 1520-1530," *Mennonite Quarterly Review* 80(4) (October 2006):501-645.

Snyder, C. Arnold, "Zollikon Anabaptism and the Sword," *Mennonite Quarterly Review* 69(2) (April 1995):205-225.

Stayer, James M., "Saxon Radicalism and Swiss Anabaptism: The Return of the Repressed," *Mennonite Quarterly Review* 67(1) (January 1993):5-30.

Weaver, J. Denny, *Becoming Anabaptist*, second edition, 2005, Herald Press.

Yoder, John Howard, *Anabaptism and Reformation in Switzerland*, 2004, Pandora Press.

Ziegler, Donald J., editor, *Great Debates of the Reformation*, 1969, Random House.

Illustration credits

Title page—Conrad Grebel's signature from the Letter to Thomas Müntzer. Public domain.

p. 2—Zürich in Roman days. Johannes Balthasar Bullinger, 19th century. Public domain.

p. 5—Grünigen Castle. ©Wikipedia User:Roland Zh. CC-BY-SA-3.0 (http://creativecommons.org/licenses/by-sa/3.0/).

p. 7—Map of Switzerland. (Modified) ©d-maps.com. Used by permission. http://d-maps.com/carte.php?num_car=24766&lang=en.

p. 8—Zürich aerial view. Derived from "2011-06-14 08-28-37 Switzerland Kanton Zürich Zürich Saatlen" by Hansueli Krapf, used under CC-BY-SA 3.0 (http://creativecommons.org/licenses/by-sa/3.0/legalcode). Grayscaled and licensed under the same license by Mike Atnip.

p. 11—Vadian. Unknown artist. (Probably) Public domain.

p. 12—Conrad Grebel house. © Dean Taylor. Used by permission.

p. 13—Conrad Grebel plaque. © Dean Taylor. Used by permission.

p. 15—Oswald Myconius signboard. Public domain by Hans Holbein the Younger.

p. 16—View from Mt. Pilatus. (https://www.flickr.com/photos/morloy/10678112185/) by Timo Horstschäfer is licensed under CC-BY-2.0 (http://creativecommons.org/licenses/by/2.0/legalcode).

p. 21—Yersinia pestis. Rocky Mountain Laboratories, NIAID, NIH. Public domain.

p. 22—Black Death. US Center for Disease Control/Dr. Jack Poland. Public domain.

p. 34—Murerplan of Zürich. Jos Murer (1530-1580), 1576. Public domain.

p. 40—Ulrich Zwingli statue. © Benuel Lapp. Used by permission.

p. 45—Grossmünster chapel. Public domain.

p. 51—Map of Zürich. S Vögelin. Public domain.

p. 58—Andreas Castelberger. Art by Peter Balholm; copyright © Rod & Staff Publishers. Used by permission.

p. 68—St. Peter's chapel. © Benuel Lapp. Used by permission.

p. 70—Iconoclasts. Heinrich Thomman. Public domain.

p. 77—Zürich debate. Heinrich Thomman. Public domain.

p. 95—Bundschuh. Unknown woodcut, 1539. Public domain.

p. 96—Thomas Müntzer. Christoffel van Sichem (1581-1658), Public domain.

p. 97—Andreas Carlstadt. Unknown, from about 1541. Public domain.

pp. 104-105—Stamps. Public domain.

p. 106—Martin Luther. Lucas Cranach the Elder (c. 1472–1553). Public domain.

p. 119—Debate. Heinrich Thomann. Public domain.

p. 122—Baptism. By Lisa Strubhar. © Sermon on the Mount Publishing.

p. 125—Manz's mother's house. © Benuel Lapp. Used by permission.

p. 126—Mission map of Switzerland. (Modified) ©d-maps.com. Used by permission. http://d-maps.com/carte.php?num_car=24766&lang=en.

p. 136—Left turn sign. Public domain.

p. 128— Interior of St. Gall chapel. Derived from "St.Laurenzen-Mittelschiff" by Wikipedia user MCvP, used under CC-A-SA 3.0 Unported (https://creativecommons.org/licenses/by-sa/3.0/legalcode); grayscaled and licensed under the same license by Mike Atnip.

p. 140—Hubmaier. Christoffel van Sichem (1581-1658). Public domain.

p. 146—Anabaptists being hunted in woods. Heinrich Thomann. Public domain.

p. 154—Prison escape. Heinrich Thomann. Public domain.

p. 157—Maienfeld. Wikipedia User:Parpan05. CC-BY-SA-3.0 (http://creativecommons.org/licenses/by-sa/3.0/).

p. 159—Manz plaque. © Benuel Lapp. Used by permission.

p. 161—Zwingli's death. Karl Jauslin (1842-1902). Public domain.

p. 161—Location of Zugerberg. Derived from "2011-06-14 08-28-37 Switzerland Kanton Zürich Zürich Saatlen" by Hansueli Krapf, used under CC-BY-SA 3.0 (http://creativecommons.org/licenses/by-sa/3.0/legalcode). Grayscaled, cropped, and licensed under the same license by Mike Atnip.

p. 165—Blaurock whipped out of town. ©Mike Atnip. Used by permission.

Series

Also in the Cross Bearers Series:

I Appeal to Scripture!
The Life and Writings of Michael Sattler

by Andrew V. Ste. Marie

Look for these future titles:

Jakob Ammann
David Zeisberger
and more!

Also by Andrew V. Ste. Marie
Walking in the Resurrection: The Schleitheim Confession
in Light of the Scriptures

I Appeal to Scripture!: The Life and Writings
of Michael Sattler

Also by Mike Atnip
The Birth, Life, and Death of the Bohemian Revival
Handmaiden of the Lamb: The Story of Anna Nitschmann
Scenes from the Life of David Zeisberger

These titles are all available from:
Sermon on the Mount Publishing
P.O. Box 246
Manchester, MI 48158
(734) 428-0488
the-witness@sbcglobal.net
www.kingdomreading.com

SERMON ON THE MOUNT
P U B L I S H I N G

Write to your friends with a memorial of one of the most significant moments in Anabaptist history!

The cover art of this book, depicting one of the most important events in Anabaptist history, is now available as a *full-color* postcard. Order from Sermon on the Mount Publishing.

"After the prayer, Georg Blaurock stood up and asked Conrad Grebel in the name of God to baptize him with true Christian baptism ..."